YOU CAN HAVE IT ALL

THE ART OF WINNING THE MONEY GAME AND LIVING A LIFE OF JOY

BY ARNOLD M. PATENT

CELEBRATION PUBLISHING
BOX 336
PIERMONT, NEW YORK 10968

Dedicated to my wife, Selma whose love and support prepared me to write this book and whose suggestions and editing brought it to life.

ACKNOWLEDGMENTS

There are many people I wish to thank for their contribution to the writing and publication of this book:

Leonard Orr for presenting ideas that led me to believe I could totally change my life; Jim Morningstar for encouraging me to present my ideas to the public; Josh Pokempner for his suggestion to write a book and for his support in organizing my first large workshop; and Tom Keelin for key insights in the use of the intuitive dialogue method.

Ann Karp for typing the many drafts of the book; Jeff Volk for proofreading and helping with the prepublication edition; and Katharine Deleot for proofreading the current edition.

Selma Bokor for editing the current edition.

Steve and Donna Schwartz for the care given to the publication of all editions.

Patricia Horan for her article about me in *New Realities* magazine and for introducing me to Jim Bolen, editor of *New Realities* magazine.

Jim Bolen for his invaluable support.

The organizers, coordinators and participants of my workshops who have taught me so much and supported me so generously.

A basic principle is that the Universe is a mutual support system. My preparation for writing this book and the direct support I received in bringing it to completion is a tribute to that system. I am fortunate that I have been trained to receive huge amounts of love and support by my family, who continue to shower it upon me. Expanding on that model makes the rest easy.

TABLE OF CONTENTS

INTRODUCTION

Tacked up on the wall facing me, where I write and work is the Latin phrase, *veritatis simplex oratio est.* Translated, it means truth is simple. I was reminded of this phrase when I first met Arnold Patent. This became even more evident as I attended his workshop and experienced the way he teaches the simple but powerful truths and laws of life.

Here is a man who, after practicing real estate law successfully for many years decided to change careers. Here is a man who does what he loves to do, does it superbly and in doing it helps others do what they love to do!

As you read this book you will learn that you are the only one who determines the path your life takes. *YOU CAN HAVE IT ALL* is an excellent road map to lead you on a joyful journey.

James Bolen
San Francisco, California
June, 1984

1

ABOUT THE BOOK

This book deals with the basic laws (principles) of the Universe. These principles have been recognized for many years but relatively few people know them and even fewer use them in their daily lives. The purpose of this book is to acquaint the reader with these principles and then to describe ways in which they can be used to increase the quality of life.

The principles are simple and easy to understand. Benefitting from them requires first, a belief in their validity, and second, a clear intention to use them. This book describes the principles in easy to understand language and explains simple ways to use them.

The material in each chapter is related to the material in every other chapter. Thus, reading the entire book will add to the understanding of each chapter.

To obtain maximum benefit from this book, it is suggested that you re-read it several times.

I have taken the liberty of alternating the use of male and female pronouns. Words synonymous with God are capitalized.

HOW IT STARTED

Each morning when I woke up, I did exactly what I thought I was supposed to do. In practicing law, which I did for more than twenty-five years, I struggled to deal with my clients' problems and with real estate investments. It is true that I created the money to live the perfect life in an affluent suburb of New York City, but what a price I paid!

The perfect life, instead of bringing me joy, brought only pain, which I carried with me all of the time. Clinically, doctors found nothing wrong with me. Yet, so great was my discomfort, that I began a search for a way to make myself well.

I started by taking vitamins and changing my diet, but it didn't seem to help. With my focus on diet and vitamins, I came across a very sophisticated nutritional program, which intrigued me and I flew to Chicago to learn more about it. During four days of intensive study, I decided to go on the program. I took at least a hundred pills a day including vitamins, supplements, digestive enzymes, glandular stimulants, etc. After being on the program for a while, I noticed that I felt better and I stayed on the program for a year and one half.

The most significant part of the program, though I didn't realize it at the time, was a daily regimen of meditation, based on the belief that stress was the single most destructive factor in one's life, and that meditation was the single most effective and beneficial way to deal with it.

I immediately began meditating, and continued for the full year and one half that I remained on the program.

It was at this point that I discovered, what were for me, new ideas. What were these new thoughts that so fully captured my attention and my imagination? They were what I call the basic laws of the Universe. These are the principles, known for many, many years, that explain how the Universe works. They are simple, straightforward and very easy to understand. However, since they are contrary to the teachings of our society, they are generally ignored.

Having learned how to accept challenges as a lawyer, investor and business person, I was now ready to undertake what seemed like my greatest challenge — adopting these principles as my day to day guidelines. And so began the second chapter of my life.

I applied the same perseverance to the practice of these principles as I had applied to the nutritional program, and noticed even further improvement in the way I felt. By this time, the discomfort in my body was greatly reduced, yet I realized that I was far from rid of it. I really began to appreciate how much pain I had experienced all these years. No wonder I had so often been uptight, jumpy, impatient and unhappy.

When I started to follow the new thought program, I discontinued the nutritional program. Not only did I sustain the improvement I had achieved, but I continued to improve. The improvement has continued, with every indication that it will do so until every last bit of discomfort has been released from my body.

I began to share the ideas with others who were interested. I soon realized that my way of stating and explaining the principles was very clear and convincing, in part, due to my legal training and experience. After all, I had been trained to apply a body of legal principles to an endless variety of factual situations. All that had changed was the body of principles.

In any event, I was encouraged to continue to present these ideas to others. Before I realized it, I had created a program utilizing many of the principles, to which a friend gave a title, "Money Mastery". This first program was a correspondence course offered to people in different parts of the country. The same friend who named the program and who was so supportive of me as I expanded it, suggested that I offer a workshop to promote it. After leading my first workshop, I realized that I had found my ideal vehicle and outlet.

Starting with evening workshops that lasted about two and one half hours, I finally adopted the full weekend format, Friday evening 7:00-10:30 P.M.; Saturday 9:00 A.M.-6:00 P.M.; and Sunday, 10:00 A.M.-6:00 P.M. I so enjoy these weekends, the material I present at them and the people who participate in them, that I am re-creating them in this book as a way of sharing them with more people.

THE WEEKEND BEGINS

Selection of the room is important. I favor one that is light and airy and that affords space to conduct part of the program outdoors in mild weather. After a short period of registration, often with live music in the background, the workshop begins. People generally sit in a circular arrangement, depending on the shape of the room and the number of participants. Their ages and backgrounds vary greatly, from 6 month old infants to 80 year old youngsters. Collars of all colors from white to blue and all those in between; college professors to academic dropouts; rich and poor, artisans, professionals, musicians and actors attend the workshops. It is so exciting to watch this broad cross-section of people so quickly and easily become a family for the weekend, freely offering support of all kinds to each other.

A workshop typically starts with a live musical presentation. The talking starts when each participant is asked in turn, to introduce herself to the group, telling her name and what she would like to gain from the workshop. This gives everyone a chance to sense the direction that the workshop will take during the weekend.

Since I do not use notes, I rely on the needs, desires and energies of the participants to direct me in the presentation of the materials. Though the basic material covered is the same, I remain intrigued with the uniqueness of each workshop and allured by the ways in which the next one will vary from its predecessors.

The more ways a person can hear or experience the same material, the more deeply it is integrated. Until the ideas become integrated, the person feels little impact.

So, dear reader, picture yourself as part of a circle of fifty or more friends and say out loud, or to yourself, what you would like to learn from reading this book. Since my workshops are largely an intuitive experience for me, I am picking up your energy, and hopefully I will present the material in a way that will satisfy your inner need.

While the material is ostensibly presented from mind to mind, I do like to ease its reception by offering a lot of live music, games and movement during the week-end. Please read small amounts between breaks. Listen to music, take a walk, or do some exercises every hour. To encourage you, I'll offer reminders.

Now we are ready for the workshop to begin. Settle in your chair. Feel the energy of the others in the circle and remember, *you know all of this material already*. I am just giving you an opportunity to review it.

I usually start at the same place — with the concept of energy.

ENERGY

Everything in the Universe is a form of energy. Mastery of money, or anything else is mastery of energy.

Energy occurs in two states - materialized energy and unmaterialized energy. The things we see around us such as cars, houses, books, and trees, are examples of materialized energy. All energy that is not in materialized form comprises the balance of the energy in the Universe. For purposes of this book, it will be defined as unmaterialized energy.

Both states of energy are more similar in form than appears to the naked eye. Even those objects which seem most solid, such as steel beams and concrete walls, appear as molecules in motion when viewed under high power microscopes.

How does energy reach its materialized form? In a most surprisingly simple way — through the mechanism of thought. Whatever we see around us was at some prior time a thought. Another way to express this is to say that we create with our thoughts.

This places each of us in an extraordinarily powerful position. However, to benefit from this power we must first believe we have the power, and then we must use it in beneficial ways.

What else do we know about energy? It is in infinite supply and available to everyone all of the time. There is an Intelligence behind it and it follows very definite laws.

We are influencing energy all of the time, since we are thinking all of the time. This is true whether or not we are consciously aware of our thoughts. Psychologists tell us that we have upwards of 50,000 thoughts each day. Most of them are the same as the ones we had the day before.

The majority of our thoughts are in the form of thought structures or beliefs. These are our programs, our preconceived ideas for interpreting the world around us; the criteria or standards by which we decide how to function, how to behave and how to react.

The difference between a random thought and a thought structure or belief, is the difference between any random event and an event or experience that has meaning to us at a deep feeling level. This determines the way we view the world. Our beliefs, which are really deep feeling experiences, are responsible for the quality of our lives. As we change our beliefs, we change the quality of our lives. It is essential that we appreciate the significance of feeling. It is the feeling behind the thought that gives the thought its power.

An important aspect of thought is that we are free to have any thoughts we wish at any time. This flows from the concept of free will, or free choice, an underlying principle in the Universe.

In summary then, we create our lives with our thoughts supported by feelings. Since there is no limit to what we can think and feel, there is no limit to what our life experience can be.

EFFORTING

In order to better understand how we utilize energy, it is important to understand the concept of efforting. Efforting is using our own energy in contrast to using the energy of the Universe. When we are in alignment with the Universe, we are functioning in accordance with the basic laws of the Universe, and the infinite supply of universal energy flows through us. When we are out of alignment, we shut off this supply of energy and require energy from our own bodies to sustain us and our activities. Efforting is the expenditure of our own energy to resist the natural order of the Universe. Efforting is the result of the belief that we are the source of our own energy and power and that our conscious minds are smarter than Infinite Intelligence.

Mastering energy requires us to surrender to the Infinite Intelligence of the Universe and relinquish the belief that we know more than Infinite Intelligence. To master energy, we must relinquish the use of our rational, conscious minds in favor of our intuition.[1] I recognize that this may be a radical statement for some of you, but bear with me and you will see the reason for it.

I can suggest a mental picture to remind you of the infinite supply of energy that is always available to you to create whatever you desire. See yourself in a sandbox at an ocean beach. Your sandbox is filled with sand and there are miles of sandy beach in three directions. You give pails of sand from your sandbox to passers by. As your supply is depleted, you reach out and refill the box with the unlimited supply of sand that is all around you.

See and hear someone coming to play with you in your sandbox. Watch him take all of your sand for himself as he plays with it. See yourself walk out of your sandbox and play on the beach with the unlimited supply of sand all around you. A few feet away the waves of the ocean splash on the sand. You can take as much water as you desire to make anything you wish out of the sand. You can make cars, houses, airplanes, tennis racquets — whatever comes to mind. This picture can also help you reinforce your belief in the natural abundance that is all around you. The more abundance you see and acknowledge in your life, the more you will experience.

———————

After a topic is presented, I ask for questions from the participants, and I shall use that format in this book. Think of your friend sitting alongside of you as the questioner. He raises his hand, is recognized and asks the following question.

Question: What is the difference between our own energy, and the energy supplied by the Universe, which you say is in infinite supply?

Answer: The energy which we create ourselves is generated from the food we eat, from what we call nervous energy and from thoughts we perceive as requiring action. For example, we are afraid of not having food, clothing and shelter, so we take a job. We wish to avoid being called lazy, so we study for exams.

In contrast with the above, consider some of the ways in which the infinite supply of universal energy is available to us. First, to avail ourselves of this supply of energy we must be comfortable in our bodies, that is, relaxed and at peace. Then we must be thinking or acting, and feeling in alignment with universal principles, such as abundance, perfection, harmony and love.

Thinking thoughts that are in alignment with the Universe and Its purpose, being in a feeling state that is similarly aligned, and acting in ways that place us in such alignment, opens us to the inflow of an infinite supply of universal energy. As we tap into universal energy, we can feel it course through our bodies, creating a sense of vitality and joy. This is how it feels to be fully alive.

You, the reader, may now be wondering, "When I am fearful, anxious, or angry, how do I achieve a state of peacefulness, and open myself to this infinte supply of energy?" The book addresses this question. As you read on, this will become more apparent, as ways to deal with these situations are described.

At this point, I wish to introduce a thought about how the Universe works. The Universe is always on purpose.[2] And Its purpose, at least in part, is to encourage each of us to move into alignment with the Universe and Its purpose. It therefore never misses an opportunity to encourage us to follow Its principles. As we come into alignment with universal purpose, we experience the ease and grace of the universal supply of energy flowing through us. Conversely, when we select principles at variance with universal principles, we are literally on our own. It is then that we require our own self-created energy to support us.

Now, I'd like to introduce the concept of the Universe, this large entity of which we are all a part. Since It is our home, understanding our relationship to it is necessary.

THE UNIVERSE

The first step in understanding the basic principles of the Universe is knowing what the Universe is and how it functions. The Universe includes everything in existence from the smallest particle to the largest galaxy. Since everything in the Universe is an aspect of energy, the form any part of the Universe takes, or that all of It takes, is the result of thought.[3] The thought behind the Universe is called Infinite Intelligence or God. This Intelligence not only created the Universe at some prior time, but continues expressing the same thought in order to maintain the Universe in Its present state of functioning.

By definition, Infinite Intelligence is perfect, and thus the Universe and everything in It is perfect. Human beings, as parts of the Universe are, therefore, perfect. One of the hurdles that each of us must overcome is to believe this.

What Infinite Intelligence creates, only Infinite Intelligence can alter. Infinite Intelligence created the spirit or essence in everything we see in the Universe. Even apparently inanimate objects like rocks have an essence which is alive and is part of the real Universe. So it is with human beings. Each of us has an essence which is not subject to our control. Since we did not create life, we do not have the power to end it.

Infinite Intelligence created our essence. It also created the conscious mind, and with it, the thought process. What human beings create with their thoughts is not immutable. What we create seems real to us, but it isn't really.

The way to tell the difference between what Infinite Intelligence creates and what we create, is that what Infinite Intelligence creates lasts indefinitely and what we create has a

15

limited life. We create things like cars, houses and clothes. The Universe creates the essence behind everything in existence, which lives on after the outward manifestation of the essence changes its form and appears to die.

God, having created our essence, set in motion the parameters for our existence. That essence, left on Its own, without our conscious mind's intervention will naturally seek to experience Its oneness with Its Creator. When we allow this to take place, we experience the true perfection of the Universe. Most, if not all of the time, however, we choose to intervene, which we have the power to do. We use our rational minds to decide what to think, do, wear and eat. When any of these thoughts or actions are out of alignment with universal principles, we feel the discomfort in our physical bodies.

Having achieved mastery of universal laws so that we are truly experiencing our oneness with the Universe and everything in It, we have also achieved mastery of energy. This enables us to utilize the infinite supply of universal energy to maintain our bodies in perfect physical condition.

However, mastery of energy requires total surrender to Infinite Intelligence. In order to totally surrender, we must release all attachment to our physical bodies. So the paradox. In order to master anything in the physical universe, we must relinquish all attachment to it. This is true of money as well.

There is a constant motivation in everything to move in the direction of experiencing more of its own perfection. This is true of trees, plants, insects, and even minerals, as well as human beings.

We know that the essence of one entity can contact another. Many of us can talk to plants and animals. In fact, we are communicating with everything all of the time and are receiving responses, even though we may have no conscious awareness of the communication. Communication takes place via the energy signals we emit, which are a result of our beliefs.

The decisions we have made about life are our *beliefs*. We have no conscious mind awareness of most of them. Our beliefs determine the signals we are giving out all of the time. And these signals return experiences which are consistent with them. Thus every belief of a positive nature will return a positive result, and conversely every negative belief will return a negative result. Each will be precise in kind and nature to the belief.[4]

Since our thoughts create our life experiences, and since we have been taught that we are not perfect, our perception of ourselves as imperfect causes us to live our lives as though we are less than perfect. However, our misperception of the truth does not change the truth. Not too many years ago, most people believed that the earth was flat. That belief was a misperception. It did not make the earth flat. It just limited most people's mobility.

The Universe, created and kept in operation by Infinite Intelligence, is ever mindful of preserving Its own existence. It does this by continuously sending signals to guide us in directions that support It. In fact, being infinitely intelligent, It never misses an opportunity to encourage us to support It. This provides us with an incredible opportunity. For, if we keep an awareness of these ever present signals, we can function with total certainty all of the time.

How do we pick up these signals? Through a mechanism that each of us has — our intuition. Our intuition, which is Infinite Intelligence talking to us between our thoughts,[5] speaks softly. In order to hear it, and feel it, we must tune out the other mechanism — our conscious mind.

What are the signals? There are basically only two. When we are functioning in alignment with the Universe, we experience a sense of comfort in our bodies. When we are out of alignment, we experience discomfort in our bodies.

As infants, we functioned mostly on an intuitive basis. Our rational society discouraged the use of this mechanism, so as we advanced in age, we were encouraged to disregard use of our intuition and to replace it with reliance on our conscious mind control. The result is the replacement of

17

Infinite Intelligence with our limited, conscious mind intelligence.

Mastery of the intuitive experience, as with mastery of anything, requires first of all, the clear *intention* to master it. In order to come to that conclusion, we must first give up the belief that rational thinking is superior to intuition. Next, we must practice using our intuition. It is a very personal experience. We have to learn what it feels like, listen for it, and use it continuously. We must notice the difference between intuition and things that seem like it, but is really each of us talking to herself.

Sometimes we have an investment in a particular result, and have no interest in listening to or following our intuition. Think of yourself as a third year student at a university, majoring in science. You realize that what you love to do is create graphic design. In order to pick up intuitive signals that will guide you perfectly in your decision as to which career to follow, you will have to let go of the need to complete your course of study as a science major. Your intuition can still tell you to obtain your degree in science. However, you want to be certain that you are not influencing your choice by your vested interest in the three years you have already devoted to the science degree.

Remember, in order to master the basic laws and have your life work perfectly, you must be totally honest with yourself at all times.

An interesting and pleasurable way to experience your intuition is through creative expression. Using color (crayons, paint, chalk or colored pencils), allow yourself to express without any conscious mind control. Choose your colors and designs intuitively. It is a fascinating experience, and it will tell you a lot about yourself.

Doing a series of these artistic expressions over a period of time, you will notice a continuity in your pictures. You will also learn to trust yourself to express freely, and you will be in touch with your intuition.

Similar exercises can be done with music, dance and sports. Remember that the ideal is to express freely without use of the conscious mind. You will learn what letting go is like. This is another aspect of intuition, trusting the inherent perfection of the Universe.

Take every opportunity to practice the principles, particularly when you feel safe. Mastering the basic principles while playing tennis, painting or dancing is no less valuable than in any other context. Pick the times and places that work best for you. Remember, the Universe supports you in keeping it simple and making it easy for yourself. Avoid waiting for crises to practice using the principles. Practice them when your life is peaceful, quiet and comfortable.

Question: Would you please talk further about how the Universe creates as compared with how we humans create?

Answer: I am glad to. All creation is a result of thought applied to energy or thought focusing energy. Every time a thought occurs, it influences energy. The more intention behind the thought, the greater the manifestation that results.

Every thought has some impact in the physical universe. Everything we experience in the physical universe is a result of a thought had by one or more people.

Since everyone is capable of having any thought or combination of thoughts, the shape taken by the world around us, and all the experiences we have with it, is constantly changing. To the extent there is consistency in our thoughts, we discern patterns within our world.

Only the Universe, Infinite Intelligence or God creates what is real. What is real is the essence in everything. In humans that essence is endowed with a conscious mind.

Since Infinite Intelligence created everything in existence, whatever we create already exists. We do not really create anything new. It just seems that way to us.

Since everything has been thought out already, the perfect experience is available to us, when we are ready to accept it. The simplest course for each of us to follow is to surrender our conscious mind thought processes to Infinite Intelligence and allow that perfection to express through us. It is when we surrender to that perfection that we understand what the true creative process is all about. It is then that we are free to express from our essence, who it is we really are. It is then that life, as it was meant to be experienced, first opens up for us.

That is the state in which artists create magnificent paintings, musicians compose inspiring melodies, and ballplayers move with the grace and agility of ballet dancers.

Question: I can see how the creative process works for the Beethovens, the DaVincis and the DiMaggios. But how does it work for the rest of us?

Answer: The same way it works for them. The principle is the same. What seems to be missing for us is the creative talent to express. Yet, the difference between those people who freely express their creativity and the rest, is only a perceptual difference. Those who do not express it, believe either that they do not have it, that it isn't worth expressing, or have some similar limited thought about it. The truth is that *everyone* has at least one talent[6] that is not only worthy of being expressed, but that *must* be expressed for the individual to be at peace with himself and his Universe.

The talents each of us have are literally God given, and they are given to be *expessed*. Failure to express them results in great discomfort in our physical bodies. *The talents want out. Holding them in* requires effort and is a major way we resist the natural order of the Universe. *We hold them in at our peril and at great cost to our physical and spiritual well being.*

Just because society often discourages the free expression of our individual talents does not mean that they have no value to us or even to society. In fact, the opposite is true.

The Universe, in Its infinite wisdom, does not create talents without the corresponding need in others to experience the expression of these talents. If a musician has the inspiration to express in a totally new musical form, there are always people who will enjoy hearing music presented in that way. In truth, each of us is a Beethoven, DaVinci or DiMaggio in the area of our talent. We are each created to be a superstar. It is for each of us to locate the talent and then express it. As we express it, we learn its value in creating a life of pleasure, abundance and joy.

Question: You mentioned *vested interest* as making it difficult for us to follow our intuition. Can you give some other examples of how vested interests limit us?

Answer: I'm glad you asked that question. Actually, the commitment to vested interest is all pervasive in our society. It requires continual vigilance by each of us to notice when it is influencing our thinking and everyone else's.

We see examples of vested interest as we look at each segment of the work force of our society. Each person, be he professional, clerk, salesperson, executive or laborer has a desire, usually on a subconscious level, to have her way of making a living continue. So her thoughts will tend to support that.

As a lawyer, I remember when no fault insurance was introduced. My practice at that time did not include automobile negligence. At first, I thought I wasn't directly involved. It didn't take more than a few moments of additional thinking for me to ask myself this question, "What will those lawyers who can no longer support themselves with negligence cases do?" I realized that many of them would branch out into real estate law, my specialty.

Though I perceived the personal threat of the proposed no fault legislation, I also realized that the concept of the legislation was beneficial to the community. Society deserved the benefit of the improved thinking on the subject of insurance. I was prepared to support it. However, I noticed that my profession started producing articles and other materials explaining all the ways in which the new legislation was inappropriate. I sensed that these arguments were not being offered to alleviate the problem, rather, they were justifications, intended to terminate this new concept which was perceived by lawyers as threatening their vested interests.

The concept of vested interest is important for you as the reader of this book. You have a vested interest in thoughts, ideas and concepts that are totally at variance with many of the thoughts, ideas and concepts expressed in this book. You will have to remain continually vigilant to notice the subtle ways you will resist the introduction and then the integration of these thoughts into your consciousness.

It's time for some music, exercise or a walk. Have fun!

———————————

Welcome back. The next topic was introduced, in part, previously. It is the concept of purpose. I mentioned that the Universe is always on purpose. Yet most of us haven't ever thought about our purpose. It is now time to think about it.

PURPOSE

It is necessary for us to know exactly how we relate to the Universe, in order for us to have the benefit of the perfection of it. We do that by defining our purpose (see below). Our purpose provides us with our general connection to the Universe. It establishes us as a part of the larger picture. We no longer feel the separation from our Source. When we define our purpose, anything that happens to us, viewed from the context of our purpose, appears more meaningful. It no longer appears as an isolated event.

I suggest that you read your purpose at least once every day to reinforce your connection to the Universe and to keep your channel open to the Source of all energy and the Source of all guidance in every decision you are called upon to make.

I also suggest reading your purpose whenever something is troubling you. The troubling event or circumstance is perceived as troubling because it is viewed as an isolated event in your life. Seen against the backdrop of your purpose, your perception of it changes and so too does its effect on you.

DEFINING YOUR PURPOSE

List two of your unique personal qualities such as enthusiasm and creativity.

List one or two ways you enjoy expressing those qualities when interacting with others, such as support and inspire.

Assume the world is perfect right now. What does it look like? How is everyone interacting with everyone else? What does it *feel* like? This is a statement in present tense, describing an ultimate condition, the perfect world, as you see it and feel it. Remember, a perfect world is a fun place to be.

Combine the three prior subdivisions into a single statement.

Example: My purpose is using my creativity and enthusiasm to support and inspire others as we all freely express our talents in joyfulness, harmony and love.

THE EXCITEMENT OF PURPOSE

Part of the perfection of the Universe is that it provides the *motivating factor* and the energy to create a life of ever increasing joy. This allows you to fashion a life of such beauty that you cannot wait for the next day to begin.

There are just a few preparations you need to take to accomplish this:

Carefully define your purpose and keep it uppermost in your mind by reading it at least once every day. Develop a sense of your connection with the Universe.

Have your life be an expression of you doing what you love. This is the specific way that you express who you really are. It is you playing your perfect role in the universal scheme. You will feel yourself as part of a winning team, and each play of the game is a fun challenge. Since the game doesn't end, you can't ever lose. You just improve your skill and enjoy the benefit of the steady improvement.

Continually remind yourself of the real game and play it as often as possible. Avoid the game of illusion. When you are living your life in alignment with your purpose and doing what you love, you are automatically playing the real game.

Reinforce your focus on the real game by reading books that inspire you to continue playing it at higher and higher levels.

Be part of a support system that is devoted to playing the real game.

Use every experience you have as an opportunity to live your life as a player of the real game. Remember, *life is just a perceptual experience.* Viewing every experience from the context of your purpose and the basic laws enables you to live a perfect life every moment.

JOY ATTRACTS FULFILLMENT

If there is no purpose in your life, why live it? When you have a purpose, you live your life at another level or in another dimension. You perform out of an inner need. You express your real self. What a joy that releases!

You need only do or be what releases the joy within. All else is handled for you.

Question: Can you give an example of other ways in which my purpose can be used on a day by day basis?

Answer: Purpose has many uses. In fact, it is basic to so many things we do. If we ask ourselves how what we are about to do aligns with our purpose, we can greatly simplify and improve the quality of our lives. An event has either little or great meaning depending upon how we see it in relation to our purpose. Ideally, we see everything we do in the context of our purpose. This leads us to eliminate certain things we do, and to see other things we do in ways that give us great satisfaction.

Another thought about purpose. Whenever you consider joining with either one or more persons in a business, social group, common interest group, etc., it is most important to deal with the concept of purpose, before you make any commitments to the group venture.

A simple and effective way to deal with purpose, when considering a venture involving two or more persons is as follows:

Each person defines his purpose.

Each person compares his purpose with that of each of the other members of the group.

Each person defines the group purpose.

Each person compares his definition of group purpose with that of each other person.

Create a simple statement of group purpose that has the agreement of all participants. Unless agreement is reached on a group purpose, there is no point in pursuing the venture. The misalignments in purpose will surface later, when you are least eager to deal with them.

Ideally, life is a liberating experience. It is an opportunity to allow us to express who we really are. We are not the part of ourselves that sees the need to struggle, compete and suffer.

The simplest way to liberate ourselves is to view life from the highest vantage point. It is only by seeing life in universal terms that we feel inspired to participate in inspiring ways. Having a purpose, and feeling the inner need to express that purpose is essential to having a life of truly high quality.

If there is one concept that is central to the mastery of the other principles and to understanding how the Universe functions, it is the concept of perfection. In order to use this principle successfully, we must be willing to relinquish the belief that perfection is either fanciful or unrealistic.

PERFECTION

Perfection is a principle on which the Universe functions, and it is a marvelous principle. It enables us to deal with all aspects of our lives with total certainty.

What are some of the indications that the Universe functions perfectly? The sun furnishes just the right amount of energy to support life and it does this without depleting its own supply of energy. The earth rotates on its axis with total precision, and without any wear and tear on itself. Our planet is supplied with the perfect balance of gases in the atmosphere to support life. Each of us has the ability to perform functions beyond human understanding, naturally and effortlessly. We digest food without any conscious mind control, and make the instant complex calculations necessary to chase and catch a fly ball. We combine two cells and create another human being, all with no conscious understanding of the process.

There are countless examples of the perfection of the Universe and all the elements that It contains.

By using the highest thought, as in using the principle of perfection, we guarantee that everyone we deal with, and everything we influence will be treated in the best possible way.

How can you use this principle of perfection in your daily life, moment, by moment? Believe that you and everyone else is perfect and treat yourself and everyone else as perfect. For example, a friend has just been fired and she stops by your house on her way home. She appears angry, upset, annoyed and fearful. You can notice how she is acting and accept those actions as real; or you can disregard them. You can realize that they are expressions of her beliefs at this moment, and that behind these beliefs is a perfect human being who is capable of experiencing her perfection at any moment that she recognizes and believes in her perfection.

You can listen to her without supporting her belief in her anger and fear. You can just continue to see her as perfect. Without support for her negative beliefs about herself and her situation, she will be encouraged to release them. The result achieved will depend, at least in part, on your ability to convey a real belief in her perfection.

An interesting fact about the concept of perfection is that it is available only to those who use it. Ignorance of the concept of perfection or unwillingness to believe in it deprives one of its benefits. Conversely, those who believe in the concept of perfection receive the benefit of it.

Each of us uses standards, guidelines and criteria in the conduct of our lives and for the decisions that we continually make. Every experience we have is the result of the use of these standards, guidelines and criteria. It is impossible for us to live our lives in a vacuum. We require some touchstones to guide us. Whatever we believe determines the results we achieve. As stated in a previous chapter,[7] we create our life experiences with our beliefs.

How then do we create the best possible life experience? Simply by adopting the principle of perfection. Use it as *the* standard and replace all other beliefs with that one belief. As long as we require some standard for our behavior, why not choose the one that gives us the best results? The higher the thought or principle that we use, the closer we come to total alignment with the Universe.

Belief in perfection requires that we give up all other beliefs. We then function solely on an intuitive basis. Using our intuition is listening only to Infinite Intelligence. When we use our intuition, we must relinquish use of our conscious minds. Bypassing our conscious minds releases all blocks in the flow of energy around and through us. The result is a feeling of aliveness, the experience of perfection.

Question:	How does the human being who was created perfectly, function in such an imperfect way?
Answer:	The imperfect behavior is a result of free will. I made up a story to explain the way I see it.

The perfect intelligence behind the Universe, God, or whatever It is you believe in, had created the Universe and was down to the last detail. A meeting of the board of advisors was called to decide the final issue. Here was a perfect Universe all ready for creation. The human beings, so integral a part of it, were incomplete. How should they be completed? Was the perfection of the Universe such that everyone *had* to live a life that was perfect in the ideal sense, without any choice? Or was the human being to be given a choice in the matter? After some deliberation, the board of advisors decided that the Universe could be so much more exciting, if humans had a choice as to how to live their lives. And so the concept of free will or free choice was born.

To give validity to the concept, a vehicle had to be created so that free will could be exercised. Thus, the conscious mind was created. It remains, paradoxically, the greatest tool and the greatest source of mischief in existence.

Being totally free, we can create anything we like. Believing, as most people do, that our individual intelligence and group intelligence is extraordinary, we are continually tempted to create life experiences that are based on so-called rational thought processes. Fortunately for us all, many people are now questioning that choice. They are at least considering the advantages of using free will to surrender their conscious minds to Infinite Intelligence. This allows the inner creativity and talent that each of us has to flower into full and free expression as an integral part of the perfect Universe.

It is only our pride, egotism and vanity that keeps motivating us to try to recreate with our limited intelligence a Universe that has already been created perfectly.

———————————

One of the ways the Universe has chosen to express Its perfection is by Its gift to each of us of one or more talents. Being in touch with and expressing these talents is a key to releasing our inner joyfulness.

DOING WHAT WE LOVE

As described in the previous chapter, the Universe and everything in It is perfect. One aspect of that perfection is that each of us has been given one or more talents. When we express these talents, we are carrying out our roles in the overall plan of the Universe.

The Universe supports Itself by encouraging each of us to fully and freely express our talents. If we want the support of the Universe, we must do what It created us to do — express our talents. It is that simple. When we do that, we are encouraged by a feeling of comfort in our bodies. When we avoid doing that, we experience discomfort.

This leads us to conclude, that in order to have a life that works perfectly, each of us must be doing what we were created to do — and that is, to express the talent or talents that are given us to express.

Talents are gifts of the Universe. We do not learn a talent. Each talent is a complete gift that comes with the tools to express it perfectly. If we have artistic talent, we have all of the skills necessary to express that talent successfully. We do not become better at a talent. We just gain confidence and become more comfortable expressing the talent more fully and freely. We open ourselves, surrendering to the Universe and letting It play through us.

Expressing a talent is not a conscious mind experience. As artists and musicians, we do not *think* about what colors or notes to select. We let go of any sense of limitation. We become totally intuitive and allow the infinite supply of energy to flow freely through us. It is an experience of freedom and joy, not thought and effort.

When we release all limitations, extraordinary things happen and it is a different and unique experience for each person. When we are expressing our talents fully and freely, we experience perfection. If we could take a pill that would release all of our negative thoughts, and open us to the Universe and Its infinite supply of energy, we would express ourselves with total magnificence. In fact, we can do it now. We shall fly into joy whenever we are ready to untie our wings.

In summary then, doing what we love is our way of supporting the Universe. The Universe in turn gives us total support and encourages us to continue to support It.

The way we locate the particular talent that is perfect for us at any specific time in our lives, is to look at what we love to do. For what we love to do naturally, is what we have a natural talent to do. The two are really one and the same.

We all know what it is we love to do. However, we often keep this information from our conscious minds. Doing the following exercise will put you in touch with what you love to do right now. When you are in touch with what you love to do, you will have discovered your talent.

A SIMPLE EXERCISE TO DEFINE WHAT YOU LOVE TO DO

Make a list of the things you love to do. Limit the list to those activities that create an excitement in you at the mere thought of them. The shorter the list, the easier it is to reach the desired result.

Select the item on the list that is most important to you. Do this no matter how much you may resist picking one item. Remember, picking one, does not mean you have to give up doing the others forever.

Make a list of the ways you can express the talent you selected in step #2. It is best to do this daily. Keep a separate book for this exercise. Do not judge the ideas that come to mind as you do this exercise. Write down every idea that flows through your mind, no matter how silly or meaningless it may seem. The purpose of the exercise is to stimulate your creative mind. After doing the exercise for a period of time, you will have developed a habit pattern that will continually produce creative ways to express what you love to do. The number of ways you can express yourself by doing what you love has no limit. Using your creativity to produce these ideas is one way to experience the abundance of the Universe.

COMMENTS ON THE EXERCISE

We all know what it is we love to do. It is an integral part of us. We can, however, keep the information from our conscious minds. This is a way of withholding the pleasure that we derive from utilizing the information to improve the quality of our lives.

The pleasure from doing what we love is a deep, fulfilling pleasure. It is an expression of who we really are, our reason for being.

Question: Why must I pick one item? I love so many things. I can't bear the thought of not focusing attention on them also.

Answer: It is important to select only one item. It is a function of the efficient use of energy. As we know, the more we focus energy, the more powerful is its impact. Focusing all of our attention on one talent, we take advantage of this principle. Once we achieve a success that is satisfying, we can introduce a second talent, and so on.

There are many multi-talented people. The ones who are successful, started by focusing their attention on one talent. By allocating part of our attention to several talents, we scatter our energies and make it almost impossible to enjoy any of our talents at a high level of success.

Remember, each of us is a superstar when we lead from strength. Our strength is our talent.

If we look at the life of an actual superstar, we notice that most of the things he does are very ordinary. He is perceived as a superstar because of one thing he does extremely well. We all have a natural ability to do at least one thing on a superstar level. When we locate what it is, and do it as though the quality of life depends upon it, each of us becomes a superstar also.

The Universe created us to function as superstars. Once we believe that, the rest is simple and easy.

If there is one principle that raises more questions and has more built in resistance to its acceptance than any other, it is the next one. Unless we master this principle, all of the others are useless. Mastery of it brings the incredible power to have everything exactly the way we would like it to be. But first comes mastery of the law of cause and effect. It is a key principle in understanding how the Universe works and how our lives work.

I suggest that you take plenty of time with this chapter. It is important that you feel comfortable with the thoughts expressed in it. In fact, until you are willing to accept these ideas, it will be impossible for you to benefit from them. Here we go.

CAUSE AND EFFECT

This principle states that we *cause everything* that happens to us. There is no such thing as an accident. This principle mandates that *we take responsibility for everything* in our lives. It is a powerful principle and we gain enormous benefit, when we believe it. However, we must accept the embarrassment that comes from taking full responsibility for many things we would rather not face, including those things that appear to be the fault of others.[8]

For example, we are in an intersection collision with another vehicle whose driver went through a red light. It is easy to blame the other driver, and thus relieve ourselves of any responsibility for the collision. When we do that however, we are in effect saying that the law of cause and effect does not apply. We have relieved ourselves of the immediate embarrassment of being responsible for the collision. But we have relinquished all of the power that comes to us by believing in the law of cause and effect. For if we take responsibility for everything that happens to us, we now open up the opportunity to create life exactly the way we like it to be. Taking responsibility for the collision is, therefore, a small price to pay for the advantage that we gain.

WHAT WE HAVE IS WHAT WE WANT

Another way of describing the law of cause and effect is to say that *everything that we have is what we want*. Or, if we look around us and see what we *have*, we know that we have it because we *want* it. (As used in this book, want is syn-onymous with cause and create.)

Again, taking responsibility for what we have now is the key to releasing the power which is inherently available to us through use of this principle.

The law of cause and effect is a very precise principle. What we have, or the result we achieve, in anything and everything, is *exactly* what we want. In order to remind us of that precision, I suggest that we see ourselves as sur-rounded by 360 degrees of mirrors. Everything that we experience is a direct reflection of what we ask for.

Another way to view this is by using the concept of energy.[9] Energy flows out of our bodies like a signal or wave length from a radio or television station. Each of us emits a very precise signal. Everyone and everything in our environ-ment picks up certain of these signals. However, only those who are on the same wave length respond to them, as only those radios and television sets that are tuned to a particular station or channel will pick up the signal of the station or channel.

The result then is that we attract into our lives those peo-ple and those circumstances which are in alignment with the energy signals we emit. If we are emitting signals of anger, we attract people and circumstances that bring anger into our lives. If we emit signals of happiness, we attract people and circumstances that bring happiness into our lives. It's that simple. And it works that way all of the time, with no exceptions.[10]

WANTING DEBTS

One of the ways we tend to hide what we really want from ourselves, is in connection with our debts. Many of us have one or more debts that seem to remain unpaid or that we pay late each month. This is no accident. If we have diffi-culty paying a particular debt, we must assume that we want the debt to be unpaid or to be paid late. Invariably, if we look at the person or company to whom we owe the money, we will notice less than positive feelings toward them. In order to change the result, we must change what we want.

There is a simple exercise that you can use to assist you in making the change.

> When you are feeling comfortable and at ease, bring the person or company to whom you owe money into mind, and see yourself having good feelings about them. No matter how difficult this might be in the beginning, continue the exercise daily until you notice that you have positive feelings about them.[11] By that time you will notice that funds to clear the debt, or to pay it timely have materialized.

Remember, you always receive what you want. When you want to withhold from someone, that is what you do. When you want to give freely to someone, that is what you do. Look at the result and you know what you want.

When you avoid dealing with a situation that is uncomfortable, it does not go away. When you have a need to withhold payment from someone, the need will intensify if you disregard it. You are continuing to focus energy into withholding, so the need to withhold becomes more intense. *Remember, you are putting energy into thoughts all of the time, whether you are consciously aware of the thoughts or not.* Once you notice a negative thought pattern, such as withholding payment from someone, you have the option of releasing the negative thought about the person, or by avoiding the issue, putting more energy into the existing pattern.

The opposite of avoidance is awareness.[12] Avoidance intensifies the existing discomfort. Awareness encourages us to take responsibility for our lives and leads us to change our wants to bring us into alignment with our inherent perfection.

There is another reason to believe in the law of cause and effect. Not believing in the law of cause and effect is another way of saying that anything can happen to us at any time, and that we are completely helpless to influence what happens to us. This is a truly scary scenario, and it is a good reason to consider adopting the law of cause and effect as a standard for our lives.

Sometimes we feel victimized by our circumstances, especially when something arises which catches us unaware. This particular result might appear to be very dramatic and very extreme, but a careful examination will usually uncover many less dramatic experiences that preceded it.

The Universe is a consummate teacher. It teaches us slowly, deliberately, and with absolute consistency. Even when we choose not to pay attention to a lesson, the teaching continues. Many of us have elected not to pay attention to many lessons. The signals were clear, but we chose to disregard them. Then one day, what seemed like a dramatic event occurred, for no apparent reason. It was just an advanced lesson in a series which we had been ignoring.

The key is staying conscious of what we create. An honest appraisal of our lives will reveal our underlying beliefs to us. This awareness then allows us to change those beliefs which are at variance with the universal principles.

Remember the power that you unleash from belief in the law of cause and effect. Taking responsibility for all the embarrassing things we create is a small price to pay for access to this power.

Question: If we always receive what we want, then how do you account for people who are killed in plane crashes?

Answer: The person who changes her flight on a plane that later crashes is not someone saved by good fortune. Nor are the victims recipients of bad luck or misfortune. Each

44

person always receives precisely what she wants. And there are no exceptions.

The law of cause and effect states that we *always* receive what we want. The tricky part is that *most of our wants are on a less than conscious level*. Remember, wants are a result of beliefs. Many of our beliefs are acquired under circumstances that cause us to suppress them immediately after we adopt them.

Thereafter, we don't remember where they came from — in fact, we aren't even consciously aware of many of them.

There is only one foolproof way to know what we believe. That is to look at the result that we achieve. Then we know exactly what our beliefs are. Stated another way, in order to know what we believe, look at what we have.

Let's look at how the law of cause and effect applies to infants. We were taught to believe that infants do not think much. We were also taught that fetuses certainly do not think. Yet modern science and technology has demonstrated, through use of sophisticated equipment, that even fetuses make decisions.

Everyone, at least from conception responds to her environment and makes conscious mind decisions about it continuously. Each of us draws different conclusions, for example, brothers and sisters raised by the same parents and with the same instructions interpret them differently.

Consider a fetus that experiences constant fighting between its mother and father. The tension during the gestation period is interpreted by the fetus as a normal condition. It generalizes that life is a tense and painful experience. It is not by accident that after birth this infant attracts circumstances and people who keep the tension and pain alive.

Another fetus, having a similar gestation experience can decide that tension and fighting are to be avoided at all costs. After birth this infant, by focusing on peacefulness attracts events and people into its life that support it in experiencing peacefulness. Other than peaceful experiences just strengthen its resolve to have a life of peacefulness.

Each of us is a complex package of beliefs. We have a multitude of beliefs and many are interrelated. Thus it is virtually impossible to sort them out on a conscious mind level. We can, however, notice what result we achieve. This tells us clearly what we want.

I have an observation to share. It is based on years of experience with many people. What I notice is that these people who believe in the law of cause and effect and use it, experience remarkable improvement in the quality of their lives. These are the people who say, "Yes, I am responsible for my life. I have the power and ability to change the negatives into positives."

Those who focus on the extreme situations are the very people who avoid taking responsibility for their lives. These are the people whose lives do not improve in any significant way.

For those who still have doubts about the law of cause and effect, I have the following suggestion. Just assume that it does apply. There is no way you can hurt yourself. For if the law does exist, you gain the benefit of believing it. If it doesn't, you lose nothing.

Not believing it means that anything can happen to you at any time. There is no way to protect yourself against such a situation, no matter what you do or believe. At least you know you haven't failed to improve the quality of your life because you didn't give yourself the chance to improve it.

It is time for a break. Put on some music, do some exercise or take a walk. When you come back we'll talk about a topic close to the hearts and pockets of most of us — money and material wealth.

ABUNDANCE

When dealing with money or any other aspect of the material world, the highest thought that we can use is the principle of abundance. The highest thought always includes and encompasses all lesser thoughts. So, using the highest thought enables us to take care of everyone and everything in a perfect manner.

ABUNDANCE IS OUR NATURAL STATE

What do we know about abundance? It is an aspect of perfection and is the natural state of the Universe. To have abundance in our lives requires a willingness to recognize that it is always available and we need only open ourselves to receive it. Stated another way, to *experience less than abundance in our lives, we must actively resist it*. To do this requires effort[13] — the expenditure of our own energy.

An example is believing that abundance is achieved by holding a job we do not enjoy, but which pays well. Many people assume that to earn as much money as they would like to have, they must do work they do not like. The unhappy result of this belief follows from a misperception of the basic principle involved.

How do you use the principle of abundance to your benefit? When you choose to make doing what you love the core experience in your life, you move into alignment with the Universe. Immediately, the infinite supply of energy is available to you. You feel the aliveness that comes from having the unlimited energy of the Universe flow through you. This aliveness influences the energy signals you emit, and the people and circumstances that will support the continuation of your feeling of aliveness are attracted to you. The experience is self-supporting.

ENERGY AND ABUNDANCE

Since everything in the Universe is energy, abundance is also an expression of energy. Mastery of energy is mastery of abundance. It works as follows. As we do what we love *because we love to do it*, we channel energy into creation of high quality products and high quality services. The people whom we attract are the ones who will support us in maintaining that level of energy and who want to enjoy the experience of that quality of energy. These are the people who will buy our products or use our services and will be happy to pay us well for them. Who would not enjoy purchasing a product or service offered by someone whose primary motivation is the joy received from creating it? The quality is assured.

Just think of owning an automobile that is built by a mechanic who loves to build automobiles. He selects and installs each part with care. The finished product is his pride and joy. Who would not consider it a privilege to own such an automobile?

The amount of energy we allow to flow through us is related to our willingness to be in alignment with the Universe and to support It by doing what we love. The more perfect our alignment, that is the more perfectly we allow ourselves to express fully and freely what it is we love to do, the more energy we allow to flow through us, and the more abundance we experience.[14]

RECOGNIZING OUR ABUNDANCE

There is another aspect of abundance that is important to understand. Much of the abundance that we think we desire,

50

we already have. Take our bodies, for example. They are extraordinary instruments with literally unlimited potential. Whatever we *believe* they are capable of doing, they can do. We limit them only by our limited beliefs about their capabilities.

At the present time we have a remarkable array of abundance in the people we share with, the food we eat, the clothes we wear, the housing we enjoy and the transportation available to us. The tendency, however, is to take what we already have for granted, and to notice only what we do not have and what we think we would like to have.

WHATEVER YOU THINK ABOUT EXPANDS

This leads to another basic principle. *Whatever you think about expands.* By noticing the abundance you already have, you receive more. By noticing what you do not have, you attract more scarcity. Use of this principle is illustrated by the following example. Assume you have $100.00 cash in your pocket and $500.00 in debts. Most people tend to focus on their debts and this causes the debts to expand. By focusing on the $100.00 and taking all attention away from the debts, the $100.00 will expand. Soon there will be more than enough to pay all of the debts. The focus on the $100.00 or the abundance you already have places you in alignment with the natural abundance of the Universe. It places you in the frame of mind to express what it is you love to do. This channels energy through you to create whatever you desire. It also attracts those people who will respond supportively.

GRATITUDE

Focusing on the $100.00 in your pocket is also a reminder of the part of your life that is working, and a reminder of what you have already received from the Universe. This encourages you to think of all the other things you already have, such as friends, food, clothes, trees, books, music and museums. Since *what you focus your thoughts on expands*, you will receive even more. The process is accelerated by expressing *gratitude* for all of those things you have already received.

DEBTS AND GIFTS

We can also change our negative concepts about debt by viewing it from its positive aspect. Debt is not the beginning of a transaction. It is invariably the second part. The first part involves receiving something, such as clothes, a car or a television set. Perhaps we borrowed money to pay for these things. In this case, we first have the opportunity to use what we bought for our benefit or pleasure.

Continuing with this approach, it is beneficial to us to see the payment of the debt as a gift to the person who originally gave something to us. It is fun to give. When we give a birthday present to a friend we feel good. Paying a debt should be no different. When it isn't fun to pay a bill, we wish to withhold love. The only way to change this is to practice feeling good about the creditor. As our thoughts about the creditor improve, so does the flow of money to pay the bill.

Again, I caution you not to be fooled by the basic simplicity of this idea. It is not only simple. It works!

When we enjoy paying bills, and this includes paying taxes, we know we are achieving mastery of this principle.

All of life is meant to be fun. When it isn't, we are withholding love from others, and from ourselves.

Question: Since abundance is our natural state, why do so many people struggle to achieve it?

Answer: If our belief is that we have to struggle to attain certain things, particularly material wealth, then the only way we shall achieve what we want is by struggling.

I was just such a believer. In fact, my belief in the need to struggle to attain material wealth was so strong, that I noticed two significant facts about my behavior. During twenty-five years of earning a living, most of the material wealth I achieved was created in less than five percent of the time I devoted to my career. The rest of the time, I literally created problems and obstacles that I had to overcome, so that the ultimate, successful result would be properly earned.

After I made the shift to doing what I loved, I blocked the flow of money because doing what I loved didn't allow for struggle. I didn't realize I had struggle and material success wired together. When I eliminated the struggle in favor of fun and feeling joy, I also eliminated the financial success which was part of the package. Finally, I allowed fun and financial success to join one another.

The principle that *we always receive what we want or believe* is relentless. It is in constant operation whether we notice it or not. People who struggle for a living, doing things they dislike, perceive the world around them at variance from the ease and simplicity which is open to them.

A related issue is one that many people have trouble with. It is a superstitious belief that in order to have some things in our lives that are good and positive, we have to be willing to accept things that are bad or negative to attain a balance. This creates a continual block to progressing in any real way with the quality of our lives. Is it worth it to improve some aspect of our lives if there is an unknown price to pay?

To master abundance requires us to deal with two basic issues. First, we must be willing to fully and freely express ourselves by using the talent or talents that the Universe has given us to express. Second, we must notice any beliefs which we have that are in opposition to the principle of abundance. If we are not experiencing total abundance we are literally pushing it away from ourselves.

The next topic is one that is a lot of fun to explain and to encourage people to deal with. Much of what we are involved with on a day-to-day basis involves this concept. And much of the confusion in our lives is a result of our misperception of it. So I introduce the concept of illusion, a concept not solely the domain of the magician.

ILLUSIONS

Since the Universe is perfect, anything that is less than perfect does not really exist. It is an illusion. Pain, anger and shortage are illusions. They exist only by virtue of our beliefs that they are real.

The world, as we currently experience it, is a result of common agreement among people that things really are the way we think they are. Most of these beliefs are no more accurate than earlier beliefs that the earth is flat or that the sun rotates around it.

Not too many years ago, practically everyone believed these ideas. The almost total unanimity of belief *did not make them true*! Today, we find that most people believe that inflation is inevitable, calories affect weight, jails curb crime, politicians are unreliable and armaments create national safety.

How do we tell the difference between what is real and what is illusion? An illusion is something that can change from time to time. What is real is always present.

Our essence is always present. For beneath the overlays of doubts, fears and other emotions, we shall always find the real self, which is pure love. Any time we look for it in ourselves or in others, it will be there.

How then do we master the world of illusion? Illusions continue to exist because people put energy into them. Inflation is kept alive because we think about it continually. So much energy is put into it, that it must expand. If the word were removed from the language, and no one talked about it or wrote about it, it would disappear. That is true of any illusion. When energy is taken away from an illusion, it disintegrates.

All illusions rely on thought to focus energy into them to keep them alive. The thought can be on the conscious or subconscious level. Thoughts and beliefs that we are not even consciously aware of are responsible for keeping alive many of the illusions which we experience as reality.

Whether there is common agreement or not on an illusion, it is possible for anyone at any time to release an illusion. That will happen when the illusion is recognized for what it really is. When the first person recognized that the earth was not flat and saw the illusion, it no longer controlled him. Those people who believe there is no relationship between inflation and their standard of living continue to live better on less money.

Let's examine the concept of debt as an example of how to deal with an illusion. Debts exist only because the concept is given general acceptance, and is used extensively in our society. Car loans, home mortgages and charge accounts are considered valuable vehicles for circulating money in our economy. Yet there are people who do not believe in debts, and they do not have any. Debt is not a requirement for living. Every day there are people who buy cars and houses for cash and enjoy doing it.

Debts are not an inherent part of the real Universe. If we are troubled by debts, it is possible for us to eliminate them from our lives. The people who have done this are essentially no different from you and me. They just have different thoughts about money. Thoughts that you and I can have also.

Debts are not a general condition. They are a specific condition. No matter how much difficulty we are having with cash flow, we do pay some of our bills. We do manage handling money to some extent, and whatever that extent is, it is not an accident. *We benefit those people we want to benefit and we withhold from others*. We have the capacity at any time to attract sufficient money into our lives to pay any debt that we really want to pay.

What then is the procedure to master debts?

Establish a clear intention to have more income than expenses.[15]

Notice all of the assets you have and all of the abundance in your life. Make it a habit to acknowledge and give thanks for everything you already have. Remember, what you focus your thought on expands.[16]

Eliminate the concept of debt from your thoughts. When you receive something that requires repayment, such as a loan, think of it as a gift to you. When you repay it, see it as a gift to the original giver.

If you notice difficulty in repaying a particular creditor, realize that you want to withhold from him. You must maintain total honesty with yourself at all times. Having accepted responsibility for withholding from that creditor, you then change your thoughts about him. Bring that person or company into mind from time to time and see yourself having positive feelings about him. Practice this until you notice that your feelings about the creditor improve. Then, the cash flow to pay the obligation will also improve.

Question: Can you talk more about the result I can expect when I release my belief in an illusion, but others around me continue believing in the illusion?

Answer: Your question points up two aspects of our lives. We function as individuals, experiencing life consistent with our personal beliefs. We also function as part of a society which has beliefs. When the individual and group differ in their beliefs, the result is interesting.

To simplify the answer, it is possible for an individual to experience total serenity and peacefulness in the midst of chaos. The more chaotic the group experience, the more deeply must the individual have mastered peacefulness and serenity.

Though each individual can achieve peacefulness on his own, the impact from the world around us is always felt. We can mute the impact by the level of our personal consciousness, but we cannot totally avoid it, nor should we be able to do so.

As human beings, we are part of a mutual support system.[17] And it is our role to support others who are interested in reaching the best of which they are capable. So our role is always dual: improve the quality of our own consciousness, and support others in improving the quality of their consciousness.

Many of the principles involve paradoxes. The next concept is one of these. The paradox of this principle is that to truly have something, we must release all attachment to it.

NON ATTACHMENT

Noticing the way the Universe functions and using It as a model leads us to conclude that the ideal state is freedom of movement. Air moves freely through the atmosphere. Water flows freely down rivers and streams. Waves roll freely onto beaches. The earth moves freely on its axis. So it is with the affairs of humans. Allowing things to flow freely in our lives gives us the maximum benefit from each experience.

Looking at it from the viewpoint of energy, we know that energy requires free movement in order to function effectively and efficiently. The energy of the Universe wants to flow freely through us. When it does, it creates the maximum benefit for us and for all who come in contact with us. Whenever we interfere with the free flow of energy, we reduce the abundance that we experience, proportionately. Blocking the flow of energy also results in discomfort in our bodies, as that is the way the Universe signals us that we are out of alignment.

One of the ways we interfere with the free flow of energy is holding on to what we already have. We hold on to money or other things of material value. We hold on to people that we have a relationship with. Holding on to anything — people or material goods — blocks the free flow of energy around our experience with the person or object (car, house, clothing or bank account) and reduces the pleasure we experience. It also inhibits the free movement of new things and new people into our lives.

HAVING DOES NOT REQUIRE HOLDING

There is a difference between having something and holding on to it. You can own a house, enjoy it and feel no attachment to it. Or you can own a house and feel that it belongs to you, and that if you give it up you are losing something. The latter is attachment. It is a blocking of the free flow of energy into your life.

You can have a relationship with a person, have a total commitment to the relationship, trust the other person completely and yet have no attachment to the person or to the relationship. You give the other person total freedom at all times. The relationship continues as a result of the participants reconfirming the relationship, constantly.

By not holding on to a relationship, there is an opportunity for other people to come into your life. Each relationship has its own kind of commitment which is special to it, and the experience of each relationship expands and enhances the quality of other relationships. In fact, while we are experiencing a particular relationship, the energies of our other relationships flow through us to enrich the present experience. If we feel a need to hold on to one or more of our relationships, we block the free flow of energy.

People tend to hold on to things or accumulate them because they feel that otherwise they might not have what they need at the time they are ready for it. In other words, they do not trust the natural abundance of the Universe to provide them with the appropriate things at the perfect time.

When we do not trust the Universe to function perfectly, It reciprocates. It continually gives us what we expect, whether it be shortage or abundance.

Holding on to things is also a result of our believing that we know what it is that we need at any time better than the Universe does. It is based on our assumption that the Universe is less than perfect. Trusting the Universe to function perfectly at all times is a key to having the benefit of that perfection.

If each of us would put more of what we own into circulation, how much more there would be for everyone to share and enjoy. Remember, that the infinite supply of energy remains available to create anything we wish at all times. The only shortage we ever experience is a result of our belief that something is in short supply or not available to us. What we are dealing with is a perception of shortage not a real one.

To prove this to yourself, think of any instance when you received something you wanted without any effort on your part, just because you wanted it.

Mastering non-attachment requires the willingness to believe that the Universe is a place of abundance and that each of us will be supported in experiencing that abundance.

It is also helpful to remember that knowing what is best for us at any time is the function of Infinite Intelligence. It is communicated to us through use of our intuition. This means that we can enjoy great material abundance when we allow it to flow freely in our lives and make no attachments to any of it.

SECURITY IS TRUSTING THE UNIVERSE

The concept of non-attachment brings up the issue of security. How do we experience security? The one way we do not experience security is by collecting or accumulating assets. Security is not something that you attain outside of yourself. In fact the person who looks to create a feeling of security by amassing material wealth is missing the whole point. Security is a feeling that comes from trusting the Universe, believing that It functions in a way that is naturally supportive of everyone and everything in It. Every time we choose to create a feeling of security by increasing our net worth, we are treating an illusion as real. We are expressing disbelief in our true security which comes only from trust in the inherent safety and perfection of the Universe.

Question: To master non-attachment, is it necessary to give up all of our assets and everything we own?

Answer: No. Having something, and owning it in the real sense are two different things. We can not truly own anything in the Universe. Nothing really belongs to us.

Our society creates a lot of common agreement on various forms of ownership such as titles to houses and cars. We are led to believe we can own things and in fact are encouraged to think we own them.

Society teaches us that success equals ownership of many things. This overlooks the universal principle that no one can own anything. The only way to truly enjoy anything is to let go of it. If you notice that something stays around, then you know it is perfect for you to experience it and enjoy it. If it leaves, you know something else is more perfect for you to experience, at this time.

Letting go in order to have is a key concept. It requires a lot of practice. It does not mean we have to divest ourselves of everything. It is strictly perceptual. It means *letting go of the perceived need to keep or own any and all of our assets.* Practice until it really does not make any difference what, if anything, you own. One of the major benefits of reaching this state is that you will not be disappointed or feel loss when the item is gone.

Mastering this concept requires mastery of some of the others, particularly the concept that we can always create what we desire with our thoughts[18]. No matter what we give up, we can replace it. It's a fun game — this game of universal principles. Everyone who plays it is a winner. It is the best and only real game in town.

As we grapple with the next concept and the principle behind it, we find ourselves also grappling with the concept of illusion. It seems so clear to us that when we give something away we no longer have it. How does this align with the principle that we only give to ourselves?

GIVING AND RECEIVING

The concept of giving and receiving is central to the understanding of abundance and other concepts such as illusion and energy. Giving and receiving are two sides of the same coin. To have a completed gift there must be a giver who truly wants to give, and a receiver who wants to receive. The giver, having given, has created a vacuum, in a sense, and is now open to receive, and the recipient is in a position to give. It is not necessary that the receiver give something back to the person who gave to her. The ideal is that both giver and receiver keep the flow going and allow everything to move freely in and out of their lives. It is the holding on to anything, the attachment, which blocks the flow.

If we visualize a circle of people and see each person giving and receiving to each of the other people in the circle, we can see how it works. When one person holds on to anything, it stops the flow in the entire circle. Everyone in the circle feels the block in the energy. When everything is moving freely around the room, everyone receives the benefit of what is circulating as well as the energy, which is circulating also.

WE ONLY GIVE TO OURSELVES

There is a principle underlying the concept of giving and receiving which further encourages giving freely to others. The principle is that *we only give to ourselves*. Remember, we are always dealing with energy which is in infinite supply. Giving energy to another person does not deplete our own supply. We can take in all the energy we desire, all of the time.

The energy flowing through us as we do what we love generates abundance for us as it enables us to create perfect products or render perfect services. The happiness we feel when we do what we love attracts the people who enjoy being around us and who are eager to support us in all ways, including purchasing our products and using our services. It also encourages people to give to us, just for the pleasure of giving.

When we deal with the concept of giving and receiving, it is important to define the term giving. A true giving, or gift, fulfills the following conditions:

> The giver sincerely wishes the other person to have and enjoy the gift.

> The gift is something the recipient wishes to have.

> There are no ulterior motives or strings attached by the giver.

When you give something for the pure pleasure of giving, and for the creation of an equivalent feeling in the recipient, you have a true gift. For the experience to complete itself requires the giver to be open to receive. The return gift can come from any source, not necessarily from the original recipient.

Think for a moment of anyone you know or knew who enjoyed giving so much, that she was the continual recipient of gifts from others. Many of us know such people. Each of us can become such a person when we integrate the principle of giving only to ourselves.

When we receive a gift from another it sets up in us an energy that stimulates us to give. This is the motivation behind the principle that we only give to ourselves. The more pleasure we feel in giving, the more energy is created in others to give in return.

Taken to its ultimate, what are we really giving when we make a true gift? We are giving love, something that is in infinite supply and is the motivating force behind the infinite supply of universal energy. Love truly makes the world go 'round. And as with everything circular, it keeps coming back.

Question: How can I best use the concept of giving and receiving to obtain repayment of a loan when the debtor is resisting repayment?

Answer: Giving with strings attached, which is what a loan is, can result in almost anything. To the extent you are attached to the money, the Universe supports you in learning to let go. The discomfort you experience is the Universe's way of telling you that what you set up is out of alignment.

The simplest way to obtain repayment of a loan, if you are ever going to receive it, is to allow the borrower to take full responsibility for the debt. As long as you keep reminding her of the debt, she is encouraged to let the repayment be your responsibility. You can give the responsibility to the borrower and say, "It is up to you to decide what you want to do about the money you received from me."

If she ever had the intention to repay you, she is now in an ideal frame of mind to feel that intention again. It is your best chance for repayment. Of course, the less you are concerned about whether she ever repays you, the more you set in motion the energy for others, not just the borrower, to give to you. Remember, the easiest way to have is to let go of the perceived need to have.

DETAILS

The Universe handles the details. This is another principle that appears to contradict common teachings.

Handling details is generally considered a conscious mind experience. It is usually an attempt to figure out the best way to function in a situation, and to plan how to achieve an objective. However, the conscious mind does not know all of the variables in any situation. Only Infinite Intelligence has this knowledge. As we relinquish this function to Infinite Intelligence, things will fall into place for us perfectly. Following our intuition, our connection with Infinite Intelligence provides us with the perfect signals or guidance without any effort on our part.

For example, each of us at some time, has had the experience of going to a place because it felt right to go there. What seemed like a chance meeting with a particular person turned out to be a valuable connection. Looking back on it, we can see that there is no way we could have planned the meeting, as the existence of the other person wasn't even known to us.

Allowing the Universe to handle the details is not a license to resign from active participation in life. Quite the contrary, it encourages active participation. When we look to the Universe for guidance for the most appropriate next step, we then proceed with certainty and are confident of success. This increases the flow of energy in and around us and makes participation in life more exciting and more fun, as well as more productive.

There is another way in which details are handled perfectly for us and for everyone else. As we do what we love, we are handling details for others. The Universe is so perfectly conceived that as we do what we love, every task is performed as an expression of some person loving what he is doing.

The Universe specializes in handling details. Allowing It to do what It does best simplifies our lives and frees us to do what we love with confidence and joy.

THE UNIVERSE HANDLES THE DETAILS

The best way I can think of to illustrate the concept that the Universe handles the details is to relate a personal experience. One evening in 1982, I gave a preview of a workshop at an apartment in New York City. A woman attended whom I did not meet that evening. She left early and did not have a chance to introduce herself. She later told me that she was impressed with my presentation and made a mental note to ask me to offer a workshop for an organization to which she belonged. It was about six months later that I received a call from Patricia Horan requesting that I lead that workshop. I agreed.

After meeting her, I learned that Ms. Horan is a writer. She told me that she would like to write a story about me for a magazine for which she is a contributing editor. A few months later, James Bolen, publisher of *New Realities* called. He decided to feature me as the cover story in his magazine. This total stranger, living on the opposite coast, introduced me to a wonderful, new audience.

At no time during this entire period did I try to reach this result. The Universe, in Its infinite wisdom, handled every detail of it. Though it is many months later, I am still in awe of the sequence of events and how perfectly they were handled.

Question: Are you saying that planning is a waste of time?

Answer: Yes. If we believe that the Universe is a place of perfection where everything has already been worked out perfectly, then our role is not to try to figure things out, which is all that planning is.

The Universe *wants* us to experience a life that works perfectly. Thinking that life is a struggle, that unless we figure things out, we will not understand what to do, are just thoughts we made up. The fact that many people think this way, does not make it true.

We can, at any time, surrender to the perfection of the Universe and allow Infinite Intelligence to guide us on our perfect path. The only precondition to this is the belief that this is how the Universe works. Believing it, makes it so! Try it! There is no other way to find out.

Question: Can you give an example of what I should do on a typical morning after I awaken, as I prepare for my day?

Answer: Ideally, you clear your mind by meditating[19] and then you do the IDEAL DAY EXERCISE. By doing the EXERCISE you focus on the quality of feeling that you want to experience during the day.[20]

Remember, we attract to us those people and events that are consistent with the energy signals we emit. When we are feeling happy, joyful and wonderful, we attract to us people and events that will sustain us in remaining happy and joyful and feeling wonderful. Starting your day in this simple way encourages such a result.

In the event you notice you are unable to achieve a feeling of joy and happiness, my suggestion is not to leave home until you do.

71

Feeling happy before you walk out of the house, no matter how long it takes, is the best investment in time and energy you can possibly make. Leaving home feeling depressed, confused or anxious guarantees that your experiences during the day will be consistent with those feelings and will just serve to reinforce them.

Question: Are you saying that I can live my life totally without planning?

Answer: Let me answer that by giving an example. Assume you start your day by creating a plan for it. You decide that at 9:00 a.m. you will have a meeting with Lucy and at noon you will have a business lunch with Harry and Mike. After your 9:00 a.m. meeting, the phone rings. It is your friend, Fred. He tells you he has just met Sam, a person who is an expert in your field and who has a wonderful connection for you in your business. Sam will be leaving town in a couple of hours, but he'd like to have lunch with you. Do you follow your preconceived plan for the day? Or do you have lunch with Sam?

The truth is that the Universe is willing, and in fact does, give us signals every moment as to what is best for us to do next. If we listen and follow Its guidance, our lives work perfectly. As you can see, this is a radical departure from how we are taught to live and plan our lives. In fact, we need not plan at all.

Remember, from our vantage point in the world of illusion, we can see only certain variables, options, or possibilities from which to choose. From the vantage point of Infinite Intelligence, all variables can be seen. If we just ask, the answer to which variable is best for us will be sent to us through our intuition, our connection with Infinite Intelligence. In the example given where a day is planned, we did not know that this excellent contact for us even existed. How could we have possibly planned to meet him?

Comment: There are times when it is appropriate to plan ahead. This is when you have an intuitive sense to do it. Your intuition in the present is telling you to do something in the future. This is not really planning.

Question: Since everyone always receives what he wants, why should we not honor the way a person expresses himself to us, be it anger, sadness, or confusion? Why look for the perfection behind it?

Answer: It is always a matter of having the quality of life that we truly desire. The way to improve the quality of our lives, if that is what we wish, is to see a situation from a higher thought level. This is what we do when we view a situation in the context of a universal principle.

Seeing past the illusion of anger or other emotions[21] that the person is expressing to the perfection that is behind it, is a choice we always have. It is a decision in favor of playing the real game. It is also the answer to the question, "Which game is more fun?"

THERE IS NO RIGHT AND WRONG

Our rational society has taught us to judge, analyze, or evaluate virtually everything we experience. So ingrained is this training, that we feel incomplete when we haven't processed each experience in this way. Yet judging, evaluating or analyzing anybody inhibits our ability to respond to the real self of that person. People are not their thoughts and actions. People are their essences which are always perfect.

LOCKING IN ENERGY

Once we evaluate, judge or analyze anything, we immediately stop the flow of energy through us. This creates discomfort in our bodies. We are then literally *stuck* with an experience the way we perceive it regardless of how it really is. Until we let go of our judgment of an experience, it ceases to be its true self and it continues to cause us discomfort.

The universal principle involved is that there is no such thing as right or wrong, good or bad. Everything that occurs in the Universe is just another event. By judging something, it becomes the way we judge it. The only way to experience the inherent perfection of anything is to see and feel that perfection.

Let's consider the following example. You cut your finger. If you view it as a bad event and become angry at yourself for your carelessness, you miss the whole point. It is wonderful that your finger hurts when you cut it. This clear signal from the Universe enables you to keep your fingers intact. It also tells you that there is a part of you, (obviously on a subconscious level) that is self-destructive, and wants to cause you pain. By having that called to your attention, you can change it.

If however, you make a judgment, you insure that you shall keep re-experiencing similar events until you learn that you are creating them.

The fact that there is nothing right or wrong, good or bad, applies equally to positive experiences. It is fine to notice that we can allow joy in our lives and it is fine to prefer joy to anxiety. But joy isn't good. It is just more fun. Each of us is entitled to a life of total joy. Let's permit ourselves to have it right now!.

Question: Since you do not believe in right or wrong, how do you suggest we deal with criminals?

Answer: One of the reasons our criminal justice system is so chaotic is that it is based on the assumption that there are such standards as right and wrong. Certain people in the society then decide what they believe is appropriate punishment for doing wrong, and they call that the law.

Belief in right and wrong negates the principle of cause and effect. If I create everything that happens to me, how can I accuse anyone of doing anything to me?

Society takes what appears to be the easy way out. In fact, it is the hard way. It is much easier to learn to withstand the initial embarrassment that comes from taking responsibility for all the discomfort we cause in our lives, than it is to try to avoid that embarrassment by making believe that our discomfort is someone else's fault.

Saying there is no right and wrong is not saying there are no *consequences* for our actions. Once we move past the concept of blame, we can then focus on what is *really* happening. If a person steals from or injures another person, even though the recipient wanted exactly what she received, the so-called perpetrator also sets in motion certain consequences for herself. There is a mechanism within the perpetrator that handles it perfectly. She cannot avoid it.

When anyone performs an act that causes pain or discomfort to another person (or for that matter, to any thing in the Universe), the consequences are direct. The performer of the act immediately feels discomfort. Though she may numb herself to the awareness of it, it will remain until she takes responsibility for the act by asking for forgiveness. She must also replace the less than loving thoughts and acts with loving ones to release the discomfort.

The law of cause and effect and the companion principle of no right and wrong encourages us to put the responsibility where it belongs. Criminals have to learn that each person is solely responsible for the quality of her life. Society is not to blame, nor is a parent, sibling, policeman, or judge.

The law of cause and effect tells us that none of us can be the victim of a criminal act unless we want to be. We control the experience of crime in our own lives. When we remove the standard of right and wrong and substitute the standard of personal responsibility, the stage is set for the quality of everyone's life to improve dramatically.

As I mentioned previously, I conduct workshops without any notes. I allow myself the benefit of as much intuitive expression as I am capable of at the time. One evening while leading a workshop, I startled myself as I heard myself express a new idea. When something like that occurs, I assume that what I am saying is accurate, and proceed as though it is. The concept I expressed was the definition of emotion. It withstood the attack of a psychotherapist that first night, and has been quietly accepted by all participants thereafter. I realize that the psychotherapist was, at least in part, voicing my own doubts about it. When he became convinced of the validity of the concept, so did I. Since it is no longer necessary for me to question it, I do not attract participants to my workshops who take issue with it.

EMOTION

Emotion is a most interesting concept. Understanding it can simplify mastery of the other principles. An easy way to understand it is to view it as an aspect of energy. The definition of emotion is the *attachment of a thought to a feeling*. The ideal, using the Universe as a model, is for energy to flow freely around and through us. Thus, the Universe intends for thoughts to flow freely through our minds and for feelings to flow freely through our bodies. Anything that impedes the free flow of either one blocks our energy and creates discomfort in our bodies, a sign that we are out of alignment.

What happens when we attach a thought to a feeling? We are labeling, describing, defining, interpreting or judging the feeling. The truth is we are defining or interpreting something we really know nothing about. Feelings aren't subject to understanding. They just are. They are like colors on an artist's canvas. One color isn't more beautiful, more meaningful or better than another. Colors just are. Yet when they occur together, each provides contrast for the others. The variety creates the interest.

So it is with feelings. One is no better than another. When, however, we perceive them as having different values and judge them, we create an energy block.

Consider the example of the friend who has just lost his job. He is on his way home and stops at your house to receive support for this unexpected event to which he is now responding and adjusting. Eager to express his feelings, he starts describing them to you. He uses words like upset, anxious, and concerned. He is interpreting the feelings he is experiencing. As he does this, he is literally stopping the feelings from flowing through his body. This creates an energy block which heightens his discomfort.

Let's assume that after fifteen minutes of this the phone rings. It is your friend's wife. She has just received a call from his employer. The company was given a very large contract unexpectedly, and has re-hired your friend and offered him an increase in pay. Needless to say, the description of the feelings that your friend now experiences will be quite different. The words used will be more like relieved, relaxed, happy, or elated.

Strangely enough, descriptions of feelings, whether they are of a positive or negative nature, have the same effect. They stop the flow of feelings through the body.

The availability of sophisticated equipment has enabled scientists to shed light on the matter. When scientists wire subjects to instruments that monitor heartbeat, pulse, respiration, body temperature, and many other physiological responses and then induce so-called emotional responses in the subjects, they find that totally opposite emotional states produce similar physiological responses.

Many events in our lives generate feelings. When we define, judge or interpret these feelings, we create energy blocks in our bodies. Learning to allow feelings to flow through our bodies without evaluating, judging or interpreting them can be a most valuable lesson.

Remember, any experience that is less than perfect is an illusion. By treating it as real, we keep it alive. Judging or interpreting a feeling is an example of keeping an illusion alive. A feeling is not subject to understanding or definition. It just *is*. As we release the description or interpretation of it, and allow the feeling to flow freely through us, we encourage the true state of our being to come forth.

What then is the absence of emotion? It is *joyfulness*. That is our natural state. Experiencing life in the context of joyfulness puts everything in its true perspective and brings us into alignment with our real selves and with the Universe.

And so, having gone full circle, we come back to the concept of perfection. If we allow ourselves to believe in it and all that flows from it, we then open ourselves to the constant experience of our natural state which is joyfulness. This is the way we express our perfection, and thus our gratitude for the incredible gifts that are given to us.

Question: If the only real feeling we have to express is joyfulness, how do you view funerals?

Answer: That is a great question and one I am eager to answer. The truth is, no one ever dies. Funerals are a game we play in our society that represents a series of misperceptions of what life is all about. The basic misperception, aside from the fact that our essence, the real self never dies, is that a person is not entitled to decide when to leave his physical body.

Infinite Intelligence granted free will for all. What right do any of us have to tell another person what to do or what not to do? Where do we draw the line? Will you allow me to tell you what color shirt, tie, or suit to wear, what to eat for dinner, what car to drive, what house or apartment to live in? Why should the spouse, children and friends of a deceased person have the right to be angry at him for leaving his physical body at a particular time? How is that different from limiting his behavior in any other way? Doing so is an infringement on personal freedom.

Society creates the sadness around funerals. Since no one ever dies, in the real sense, and since we can, if we wish, maintain contact with people who have left their bodies, why all the trauma? When a person leaves on a cruise, we throw a party. A funeral should be more like that. Celebrate a trip that is more exciting and challenging than a cruise.

The next topic addresses an issue that each of us is involved with almost continually — relationships. Improving the quality of our relationships clearly improves the quality of our lives.

HARMONY

Having a life that works perfectly requires harmony in relationships. In order to determine what harmony is, we look to the Universe for guidance. There we always find the ideal model. Since the Universe is a mutual support system, the key to a harmonious relationship is the support of the others in the relationship. How is this best done? By seeing them as perfect.

Anything less than perfection isn't real. It is an illusion. Seeing anger, confusion, anxiety or fear in another person is just giving validity to an illusion. It also encourages the other person to believe that the illusion she is presenting is real. The ideal response is to disregard the illusion that the other person is expressing and see that person as the perfect, joyful person that she really is.

The more we practice, the easier it becomes. A simple way to practice is to glance at each stranger as she walks toward us on the sidewalk. Notice her apparent facial expression and then immediately go behind it and see her as perfect and joyful. As we improve our ability to do this, we receive a marvelous benefit. We increase our ability to see ourselves as perfect and joyful.

Returning to the concept of energy, each of us emits energy signals all of the time. Everything that happens to us is just a return to us of something we have asked for — something we have signaled others to give us. To help you keep this concept in mind, remember my suggestion that you think of yourself as surrounded by 360 degrees of mirrors.

Everything that we experience is a reflection of what we ask for. The least perceptible nuance in another person's facial expression is precisely what we are evoking. This is another aspect of the perfection of the Universe. The Universe misses nothing and always gives us the perfect response to our action or thought. When that response creates discomfort, it is the Universe's way of reminding us that our perception is out of alignment. It is a signal to let go of whatever illusion we are involved in, and remind ourselves of our own, and everyone's, perfection.

PEOPLE PRESENT THEMSELVES TO US THE WAY WE WANT THEM TO

As with the concept of abundance, the way we perceive harmony in relationships, is the way we experience it. Becoming comfortable with the idea that people present themselves to us the way we want them to, is a big step toward experiencing harmony in relationships. Remember, wanting something on a conscious level is not the only way to want it. Most of our wants are expressed on a subconscious level.

When we attract a person who acts less than lovingly toward us, that person is showing us a part of ourselves that we do not love and accept. The Universe in Its infinite wisdom is giving us the opportunity to see a part of us that we are hiding from ourselves. It is by recognizing this part of ourselves and changing it, that we release the energy locked in our bodies. The discomfort that we continually experienced disappears when we can do this.

Achieving harmony in our relationships requires us first to be in harmony with ourselves. Focusing on the word harmony reminds us of our perfection and everyone else's. It brings us closer to experiencing harmony in relationships.

———————

It is time for another break. Put on some music, do some exercise or take a walk.

THE PAST AND FORGIVENESS

One subject that attracts great attention is the past, and particularly how to release those parts of it that seem to haunt us. Actually, any part of our past that influences our present is part of our present. And since only the present really exists, we can only release our present, in the present.

Any discomfort we experience is a result of locking energy in our bodies. More particularly, it is a result of attaching thoughts to feelings.[22] Something occurred in our experience which we interpreted in a way that created the attachment. This usually occurs when we perceive that another person is expressing less than unconditional love and support for us. Such a judgment stops the free flow of feelings through our bodies.

How then do we release the energy block? Stated another way, how do we detach the thought or judgment from the feeling? From my examination of the various alternatives offered, I find the simplest and most effective to be the concept of forgiveness which is really the complete suspension of judgment.

As we practice forgiving the person we previously judged, or are judging, as unloving toward us, we loosen the attachment of the judgment to the feeling. Since some of our judgments run deep and strong, we must practice forgiveness for an extended period, until we release the judgment totally.

The Universe is continuously helping us to clear these blocks. It keeps sending us people who act out the roles of those we need to forgive. Anytime we experience someone whose behavior causes us discomfort, we know that person represents someone, or is himself someone, whom we haven't forgiven. By forgiving the person in our present experience, we are also forgiving whomever that person might represent, even though we are unaware of any connection.

To take the matter full circle, the person each of us is actually forgiving is himself. Originally, someone made a judgment about our behavior. For example, we were scolded for being late for meals. At some point we adopted the belief about ourselves that when we are late for meals, we have done something wrong. Thereafter, anytime we are angry because someone else is late for meals, a part of us still wants to come late for meals while another part believes that it is inappropriate behavior.

When we are able to feel comfortable when someone else is late for meals, we know we have forgiven ourselves for coming late. Releasing the judgment of another is really releasing the judgment about ourselves. As we feel comfortable in the presence of another, we are really feeling comfortable with ourselves.

Forgiveness is another way of changing our perception of people and events. *Judging anything is a misperception of it*. Everything that occurs is just another event or experience. It is neither good or bad, important or unimportant, right or wrong.

Why not allow ourselves to see the perfection in every experience? Life is just a series of events which we have attracted, in order to see where we stand in our personal growth. Forgiveness releases the energy block and returns to us the joy which is our birthright.

Question: I am often asked how changes made by one person in a close relationship affect the other person.

Answer: When one person in a relationship changes, the other person changes also whether he consciously wishes to or not. This is a result of the operation of several of the basic principles. Let's look at a few of them. We are assuming of course, that the changes are in the direction of being more in alignment with the basic principles.

The law of cause and effect tells us that when a person *wants* a higher quality of life, he gets it. Those in the environment of one who has become more aligned, will pick up the changed energy and respond to it in kind, without conscious awareness. As an example, let us assume two people in a relationship quarreled a lot. When one of them loses interest in quarrelling, the other has no one to quarrel with.

Viewed another way, everyone around us reflects exactly what we ask for. When a person changes what he asks for, the response of those around him must change accordingly.

Consider the situation from the aspect of the principle that there is no right and wrong. The person who believes this, will stop finding fault. This will certainly change the other person's behavior.

Another principle will lead to an even more dramatic change in the relationship. That is seeing only perfection in the other person.

In summary then, any time one person in a relationship moves into alignment with the basic principles, the impact on the other must be felt in a beneficial way.

UNITY

To understand the concept of perfection, it is necessary to understand the relationship each of us has to the Universe, which is our Source, and the relationship we have to each other. Underneath all the apparent differences, the essence of each of us is not only perfect, but the same. This is inherent in the concept of perfection.

As mentioned in other chapters, we can continually look behind the projection of other people's attitudes, expressions and emotions, and notice only their perfection. This is the way we avoid dealing with illusions and master the basic principles. As we keep in mind the unity of all parts of the Universe, it will simplify our understanding of perfection.

Remember, we only believe in our own perfection when we believe that everyone else is perfect. When we see another person as less than perfect we really see our own imperfection. This occurs to call our attention to a part of ourselves that we do not love. We should be very grateful for these experiences, for as we learn to love another person, we are really learning to love a part of ourselves.

A simple way to do this is to first locate a quiet and peaceful time and place. Next, bring the person we see as less than perfect into our minds. Then see ourselves feeling comfortable in the presence of the person. No matter how difficult it might be for us in the beginning, as we practice, it will become easier and easier. Eventually, when we have pleasurable feelings about the person, we have also learned to love a part of ourselves that we previously did not love.

Sometimes we may find it difficult to generate pleasant feelings about someone. If that is the case, there is an intermediate step that is very useful. It is forgiveness.[23] This is the

89

bridge between our present feelings of discomfort about a person and our learning to unconditionally love her. When practicing forgiveness, it is important to first forgive the other person for all the things she does that we perceive as less than loving. We must, however, also forgive *ourselves* for all the things we have done that are less than loving toward that person.

Remember the length of time it takes us to truly forgive another person, or ourselves, is not important. What is important is our *intention* to finally forgive, and our *perseverance* in practicing forgiveness until we succeed.

It is also important that we remain *aware* of each time we do not forgive, and strengthen our resolve to practice forgiveness of others and ourselves. Everyone is always entitled to forgiveness. Since each of us is, in essence, a part of everyone else, we can not achieve total forgiveness of ourselves until we have totally forgiven everyone else.

An important aspect of the perfection of the Universe is that it continues to provide us with the experiences we require to become *aware* of our illusions about ourselves and others. These experiences help us to release these illusions in favor of seeing perfection in others and in ourselves.

Question: When I think of all the people I now interact with, from my boss to certain relatives and friends, I realize how much other people's behavior bothers me. It seems like an overwhelming task to forgive all of these people and learn to love them.

Answer: How successful you will be, and in fact whether it will be an impossible task, or a fun challenge, is up to you. In order to win the game of life, we have to keep asking ourselves, "What is the real game?" If we conclude that the real game is having money, assets, a better house and car, more vacations and more status and power in our communities, then forgiving anyone is virtually impossible. If we look at our purpose and the universal truths that support it, and see the mastery of them as the real game, then learning to forgive others and finally loving them can actually be fun.

Infinite Intelligence is our silent Partner as we go through life. Whenever we choose to play the real game, we notice that our Partner provides us with incredible support. In fact, just the decision to play the real game guarantees that we cannot lose.

TIME

The concept of time helps us to understand how the other concepts relate to each other. Society teaches us that time occurs in three stages: the past, the present, and the future. In fact, there is only one time that is real — the present. The past is gone, it no longer exists. The future is yet to occur. *Only the present moment ever really exists*. What we believe at any given time creates our experience at that moment. When we change our beliefs about anything, the old beliefs are gone. We function based on the new belief, as we can only have one operative belief about anything at any one time.

Our concept of time influences our perception of our experiences. We tend to see present experiences in the light of past experiences. This means that we expect things to remain pretty much the same as they were. This is especially true of the way we respond to others. We draw conclusions about the people we interact with, and the next time we are with them we have certain expectations.

Consider the following example. As you are walking down the street, you meet a friend who introduces you to the person he is with. This person is obviously impatient and pays little attention to you after he is introduced. As you talk to your friend for a few minutes, the other person waits politely, but is obviously growing more impatient and is eager to leave. You next meet this person at a party. As soon as you see him, you remember how impatiently he acted. This intrudes on your ability to find out what he is really like.

You were not aware that when you first met this person, he had just come from visiting his mother who was critically ill. He was eager to discuss certain decisions about his mother's treatment with his friend. You, without realizing it, were delaying that discussion.

Having drawn certain conclusions about this person, you now expect him to act a certain way. Your expectation about how he will act encourages him to act that way. Seeing the present through the eyes of the past is a way of remaining in the world of illusion.

In order to see another person as perfect, we have to release all of our preconceived ideas, thoughts or beliefs. However, perfection can not be experienced as a thought. It can only be *felt*.

Consciously or subconsciously, remembering how a person behaved previously intrudes on our ability to relate to the perfection of that person in the present. It forces us to relate to the illusion of that person rather than to his perfection.

This is akin to viewing a sunset. Each one is different from the ones before it. Comparing the one we are viewing with past sunsets detracts from our ability to fully experience the one we are viewing. Describing it in any way limits our ability to experience it fully.

Consider the following situation. You are in your home with a group of friends. The phone rings and the caller tells you that a man is on his way to your house. He is a very special man, a hero, who has just saved many people in a burning building, at great risk to his own life. You hang up and tell your friends about the call and about the man who is on his way. Everyone is excited and can't wait to meet him.

When the door bell rings, you welcome the hero and express your appreciation for his wonderful accomplishment. After several minutes pass, the phone rings again. It is the same caller. She apologizes for the previous call and tells you that there has been a big mistake. The man who is in your living room isn't a hero. He is a murderer. Instead of saving many people, he just killed them. Needless to say your energy and that of all the others in the room changes instantly, as you are all in fear of your lives.

Perhaps the man just wandered in from the street and is neither a hero nor a killer.

This story illustrates how what you believe at any time creates a reality for you.

When we see only perfection in someone, what we are told about him does not influence us one way or the other. He is then free to respond to us, perfectly.

Learning to be totally in the present, the only time that ever exists, is a skill that requires constant practice. We must continually remind ourselves that whatever we are presently experiencing is unique. It never happened before. It will never happen again. We are free to see it differently than we ever saw it before.

Question: Much of our lives revolve around the clock. We concern ourselves with getting to work on time, completing jobs on time, and meeting people on time. How do you suggest we learn the new concept of time?

Answer: The solution to any problem is always the same. Look for a universal principle and view it from that perspective. Stated another way, to solve a problem that you are experiencing at the level of illusion, go to a higher level of thought.

Whenever time appears to be a problem for us, one thought we can introduce is the law of cause and effect. We have created a situation for ourselves where time is an issue. By taking responsibility for creating the problem and of course not judging ourselves or anyone else for its creation, we can see how time is not the issue.

Let us make it specific. Assume your boss wants you to complete a report by a certain date. You believe he has not allowed enough time. We both know that when you truly *want* to do something, the ideas flow rapidly and easily. Obviously, for whatever reason, if you can not see how you can finish a report on time, you really do not want to finish it on time.

The one thing we know is that time is not the real issue. Ideally, you will see the real issue in terms of a basic principle.

To continue with the example, allow yourself to notice your thoughts about your boss, your job and the particular assignment. Should you notice that any of your thoughts are less than positive, meditate on them. As you allow yourself to feel comfortable, you will release your negative thoughts.

You can understand from the foregoing illustration, that mastery of the principles requires great perseverance. We must be relentless. The principles are in effect all of the time, whether we pay attention to them or not. They are available for our use, all of the time. They only work *for* us when we use them. When we disregard them, they often work against us. The choice is always ours.

EVERYTHING ALREADY EXISTS

Another aspect of perfection is that everything already exists. This is true of everything. There might seem to be something new and different than was ever thought of before, but there isn't.

Creativity is, for each of us, a new way of seeing what already exists. We use it in its highest form when we search out more ideal ways to live our lives in accordance with our purpose and the purpose of the Universe. The Universe is diligent in seeing to it that the quality of the life we experience is related directly to the quality of the objective we seek.[24]

Our thoughts (beliefs) attract additional thoughts that are consistent with them. For example, you are scheduled for a job interview as an executive secretary. You are concerned about the interview. The following thoughts cross your mind. "I will appear nervous. I will not type as well as I can because of the pressure of being judged. Other applicants will have more skills, or present themselves better at their interviews."

Since our existing beliefs continually attract thoughts that are consistent with them, our lives continue to expand in the direction of our existing beliefs.

If we wish to change our lives, we must change our beliefs. A new pattern is then generated in our lives. Let's go back to the example. Suppose that you talk with a friend who reminds you of your many and varied office skills. Your friend also tells you that you are highly qualified for the job, and the prospective employer will be eager to hire you. You think about your skills, and realize that the friend is correct. This leads to thoughts such as, "It will be fun to work for the new company. This position will give me the opportunity to use my creative writing talent." You are now feeling confident about the situation, which will lead to a favorable interview.

Question: You keep saying that we should not focus on material wealth. If we don't focus on it, how can we achieve it?

Answer: Thanks for the question. The principle involved is that the Universe is a place of abundance. For us to be experiencing less than total abundance means we are literally pushing it away from ourselves. Abundance naturally wants to flow through our lives. That is why we do not have to focus on it to achieve it. If we just do what we love and express ourselves fully and freely, we are serving others in accordance with our purpose and the universal purpose. All that is left is for us to open ourselves to receive. It is that simple.

Since this is such an important principle, let me state it another way. As long as we believe that in order to have money we must work for it, we guarantee that we shall have to work to obtain money.

Until we can *feel* the abundance of the Universe, we have to keep *reminding* ourselves that this is our natural state. We can not do this too often. When the shift in our beliefs occurs, then the shift occurs in the flow of dollars and other forms of abundance into our lives.

TRUST

As stated many times, in order to have the benefit of perfection, we must first believe it. We always experience what we believe. Our belief in the perfection of Infinite Intelligence allows us to relinquish use of our conscious, rational mind, and defer to our intuition.

Mastery of perfection is really a release procedure. It is a letting go of believing that we are less than perfect. The more we believe in perfection, the more we are willing to let go of thoughts that are in opposition to it. We are then able to trust the Universe to give us the benefits of Its perfection.

We express trust in perfection when we surrender the use of our conscious minds to our intuition; when we allow our real selves to surface and express our talents fully and freely; when we notice the difference between the world of illusion and the real Universe; when we allow ourselves to be inspired and inspire others; when we keep reaching for more exciting, more enlivening experiences; when we believe that the more we express our perfection, the more we support the Universe, and the more we inspire others to express their perfection.

As we increase our belief in the perfection of the Universe, and all that it implies, we increase our willingness to trust that we will be provided with a life that works perfectly.

Question: I understand what you are saying on an intellectual level, but as I think of leaving my present job for a more perfect one, and trusting that the natural abundance of the Universe is there for my support, I notice I don't really feel trusting. How can I bridge the gap?

Answer: This is a situation faced by many people who are trying to create positive changes in their lives. No matter how much each of us has already mastered, the next step always introduces us to a confrontation with one or more of the basic universal principles. It is a part of the game. The first thing to do is to remind ourselves of the game we are playing, and of its rules. Next, it is helpful to learn to enjoy playing the game, as a game.

One of the techniques that we have to master to play the game successfully, is trust. The only way we can truly learn a principle is to experience it. We have to test ourselves. That requires trust, which is an inherent part of the real game of life. We must keep asking ourselves, "What is real and what is an illusion in our lives? Why should we give up the illusion, if we do not believe that the Universe truly supports us?" It is only when we trust, that we experience the support.

The next step is always the same. We must notice the gap between what we believe and what we would like to believe. What do we really believe about the principles? It doesn't serve us to make changes before we are ready. By reminding ourselves, as often as necessary of the gap between what we really believe and what we would like to believe, we keep narrowing that gap. One morning we wake up and realize we have achieved our goal.

COMFORT AND DISCOMFORT IN OUR BODIES

The Universe sends us two basic signals as indicators of our degree of alignment with it. Comfort in our bodies is evidence of our being in alignment. Discomfort is evidence of our being out of alignment. The degree of comfort or discomfort is in proportion to the degree of alignment or misalignment. The signals in our bodies can range from excruciating pain to joyfulness.

What makes it most interesting is that we are always dealing only with perception. Thus it is *our interpretation of a situation, rather than anything inherent in that situation, which determines whether it will be a source of comfort or discomfort to us*. Since we attract people and situations as a result of the energy vibrations we emit, we are always in a situation that reflects exactly what we are asking for. If we view it that way, life works perfectly all of the time.

To understand the concept of comfort and discomfort we must first understand the concept of perfection.[25] We are not our bodies, thoughts, feelings, beliefs, experiences, or any of the things we own or use. We are only our essence, which is always perfect.

The extension of this concept also helps us to understand the world of illusion. Whatever thoughts, beliefs or agreements are current in the world at any time is irrelevant. These thoughts, beliefs and agreements do influence how people act and the results they achieve, but they never change the underlying perfection that is the essence of each person and the inherent state of the Universe.

Using the signals of comfort and discomfort correctly, requires that we interpret them differently from the way we were taught to interpret them. Society encourages us to believe that withstanding discomfort is essential to advancement in areas such as career, marriage, raising children, and building a secure future.

We are thus continually faced with the need to remind ourselves to view the signals in the way we intuitively want to read them. It takes a lot of practice to allow our lives to be simple, easy and fun.

A word of caution. When you choose to make changes in your life, it is prudent to provide yourself with as close to an ideal environment as possible. The most ideal environment is a support system of one or more people who will give you unconditional love and support as you reprogram yourself.

Remember, the Universe is a mutual support system.[26] Each of us has a need to function in a mutually supportive environment. Providing yourself with this environment is the key to a successful transition and ultimately to a life of total joy.

Question: I can think of many ways I can experience comfort in my body. I can drink alcoholic beverages, eat chocolate cake, smoke or watch a ball game. You seem to be talking about something else. Will you elaborate on this?

Answer: The signals of comfort and discomfort in our bodies that I am talking about are on a deeper level than the examples you gave. I previously mentioned the principle that, the Universe handles the details. Many people ask, "Then what is there left for us to do?"

We must notice on a deep level when we are feeling comfort or discomfort from the situations that life presents to us. The part of us that is real knows the difference. By allowing that part of us to become active, we learn to distinguish between the world of illusion and the real Universe. It is the same part of us that responds intuitively to the world around us. The standard we employ to evaluate it always determines the result we achieve. Using the part of us that knows what is really happening insures the best possible result.

THE SPONGE

We are not like automobiles. We cannot put our lives into park or neutral, or turn off the ignition. Our existing beliefs continually focus the energy that flows through us. If you are afraid of losing your job, you will attract circumstances that will support you in losing it.

As to the parts of our lives that we have not clearly defined, there is a risk factor of which we should be aware. In our society there are powerful forces focused on each of us all of the time. These are in the form of television, radio, newspapers, magazines, salesmen, employers, relatives, and friends. They have many ideas about what we should be thinking. When we avoid making clear decisions about what is best for us, we tend to adopt the ideas of these other sources, without being aware that we are doing it.

Our consciousness is like a sponge. We can fill it with our own ideas and decisions. We can fill it with joyous thoughts and clear intentions to have a life that works perfectly. Or, if we leave the sponge partly dry, the world around us gladly fills it for us.

The solution is simple. We can start each day with a clear intention to feel wonderful all day. This reinforces the need to do the IDEAL DAY EXERCISE regularly. We must keep the quality of life experience we wish for ourselves in our consciousness. The choice is always ours. When we avoid making the choice, others make the choice for us.

Fill your own sponge with happiness, harmony, peacefulness, aliveness and joyfulness.

Question: How does the suggestion to fill our sponge align with the principle that the Universe handles the details?

Answer: If you notice the suggestion I made as to how to fill the sponge, you will recognize that I suggest focusing on the *quality* of the day or the experience, not its details. Our role is to focus on feeling joyful and allowing the Universe to send us those people and events that will support us in experiencing the joyfulness.

NEGATIVE THOUGHTS AND JUDGMENTS

What is a negative thought? It is any thought that does not recognize the perfection of the Universe and everything in It. This definition classifies any thought which expresses a judgment, as negative. When we judge anything or anyone we confirm an illusion.

Consider the following example. You are viewing a painting. A person standing next to you asks for an opinion of the painting. If you answer based on the shapes and colors on the canvas, you are missing the creative interaction between you and the artist. It is the artist's desire to reveal and express herself to you that is the essence of her talent. When you receive that, you are best supporting the artist and yourself, and sharing the perfection of the experience. Everything but the perfection is an illusion.

Judging the painting or the artist is no different from thinking that anger, sadness or fear is real.

Brought to its logical conclusion, seeing only the perfection of everyone and everything encourages others to express that perfection. If we judge the result, no matter how excellent the product or the expression, we limit rather than encourage free expression.

Remember, each of us is here to express our talents fully and freely. Whatever encourages us to express these talents supports us. This in turn supports the Universe. Making judgments limits full and free expression of talent.

A comment for those who fear that only by judging the quality of a person's expression, can society encourage the production of higher quality goods and services. When we do what we love, we are expressing those unique qualities and talents that the Universe has given us. Our performance, motivated by the joy it generates, automatically produces the highest quality of which we are capable. This is all part of the perfection of the universal plan.[27]

WHEN WE CEASE JUDGING OTHERS, WE ARE AT PEACE WITH OURSELVES

Remember also, whenever we judge anyone negatively, we are really judging the aspect of ourselves that wishes to act the same way. Yet another part of us believes that expressing this aspect is inappropriate. Until we cease judging others, we know we are not at peace within ourselves. Stated another way, when we are at peace with everyone and everything, then we are at peace with ourselves. We make peace with others to create peace within ourselves.

Question: Please amplify your thoughts about not judging the work product of anyone. How is that truly supportive of the person?

Answer: I'll be glad to. This issue is one I remember discussing in college. It seems to be an issue that comes up often, and has meaning for many of us. If one of the basic principles is that life in its ideal form is a mutual support system, then how do we ideally support another person? Do we help the person by pointing out that her performance is less than perfect, from our point of view? We must recognize that we are only our essences which are perfect and not our work product, or our thoughts, or our actions. By

108

judging anything about a person, we support that person's belief she is an illusion of herself.

Whatever a person expresses is the closest that she is able to come to expressing her true essence which is the perfect part of herself. We always have the choice of supporting an illusion, or the real self of another person. The choice is up to each of us in every situation.

We do not encourage a person by telling her how she has failed, or how she has expressed herself imperfectly. Rather, we encourage a person by noticing all the ways she is already perfect. Since each of us is already perfect, we do not have to learn how to become perfect. All we need from each other is the support and encouragement to express that perfection.

YOUR IDEAL DAY EXERCISE

In order to achieve a life that works perfectly, we each have to decide what a perfect life is. Perfect is a word that has a different meaning for each person. If you want to have a perfect experience, you must first define it. Once you define it, you are then able to put energy into that definition, which in turn, attracts perfect events to you. This creates the experience of perfection that you have defined.

Any resistance you have to defining your ideal day is just a resistance to creating a life that works perfectly.

When you do the first IDEAL DAY EXERCISE, it doesn't make any difference what it looks like. It can be rather lifeless, dry and unexciting. As you continue on successive days, you will improve your concept of ideal. In a relatively short period of time, you will notice that you are able to conceive of a more exciting, pleasurable and joyful day. What you are doing is expanding your consciousness, and expanding your willingness to have your life work better. The more you do it, the more you will open up to the real potential of your life.

There is no limit to your potential. YOU CAN HAVE IT ALL.

Practice feeling wonderful. Expand your mind. Stretch yourself in your willingness to have a higher quality experience than you had the day before. Keep improving your willingness to experience more beauty, aliveness, harmony and joy in your life.

The ultimate function of the IDEAL DAY EXERCISE is to put us in touch with the only part of us that is real — our joyfulness. Since many of us have buried it deep within, we must continue to remove the layers of illusion that cover it, until it shines forth continuously. Each day that we do the IDEAL DAY EXERCISE, we release more joyfulness.

Remember, we are awakening a *feeling*. *Feelings* are not details. The Universe specializes in details. We specialize in *feelings*. And we have to keep reminding ourselves that only one *feeling* is real — joyfulness.

To assist yourself in locating the joyfulness within, keep in mind that joyfulness is a spiritual quality. Using spiritual concepts and thoughts in the description of your ideal day will lead you to the feeling of joyfulness within.

AN EXAMPLE OF AN IDEAL DAY IS AS FOLLOWS:

I awake feeling grateful for the wonderful rest.

I notice a calm and peaceful feeling in my body.

I am eager to start the day.

The thought of doing what I love brings a surge of energy through my body.

I am looking forward to all of the new experiences I shall have and all the love I shall give and receive.

I realize that everything in the Universe is perfect, and only perfect things happen to me.

I sense a direct connection to Infinite Intelligence, and trust that I will be guided perfectly as I use my intuition.

I am filled with joy and see myself radiating that joy to everyone all day long.

Question: Please explain how we can focus on the quality of the day, without involving ourselves in the details of it.

Answer: The quality of the day is how you *feel* as you experience the day. What difference does it make to you where you are, who you are with and what is going on, if you are *feeling wonderful*? Conversely, if everything is just as you planned it, what good is it, if you are feeling depressed?

I previously presented the concept of perfection, as what is real in the Universe. There is only one real feeling which we can experience, and that is joyfulness.

The function of the IDEAL DAY EXERCISE, and the suggestion to focus on the quality of the day places our attention on our joyfulness. We spend so little time noticing this essential part of ourselves, that it rarely comes into the light of day. By searching it out, we allow ourselves to feel it and encourage its expansion in our lives.

Remember, *when we focus thought on something, it expands*. We cannot spend too much time focusing on joyfulness.

As for the details of the day, they are always a result of the quality of the energy signals we are emitting. When we focus on joyfulness and allow it to expand within us, we attract events and people that bring more joy into our lives.

ALIVENESS

Our bodies are finely tuned instruments which are designed to function perfectly as the energy of the Universe flows freely through them. When we allow this to happen, we experience the feeling of aliveness. Anything that impedes the free flow of energy through us reduces our feeling of aliveness. As the absence of emotion is *joyfulness*, so the absence of any block in the free flow of energy is *aliveness*. The culprit which impedes the free flow of energy is the conscious mind. When we are able to trust the Universe to guide us perfectly and are able to surrender totally to it, we shall know what aliveness is all about.

We experience aliveness when we feel inspired. Inspiration occurs when we peel off uncertainty and all the other illusions and get in touch with our essence, our perfection. That is the part of us that wants to fly, to soar, to express our uniqueness in ways that enable us to feel the true joy and beauty of our real selves.

We are capable of being inspired all of the time. Believe it is possible, and then put energy into it by thinking about it often. Remember, perfection already exists. Our role is to recognize it and place ourselves in alignment with it, letting go of all beliefs that are in opposition to it.

We can always look for, notice and acknowledge our own and everyone else's magnificence. It is always there. It's fun to be magnificent and play with other magnificent people.

You can live your life any way you choose. Choose inspiration! Choose aliveness!

Question: You refer again to the conscious mind as the major impediment in our lives. Why then was it given to us?

Answer: The only way I can justify the existence of the conscious mind is that it gives validity to the basic, universal principle of free will and free choice. For each of us to make choices, we require a mechanism. That mechanism is the conscious mind.

Our society believes that use of the conscious mind is essential to improve the quality of our lives. We are taught to evaluate, judge, analyze and interpret everything. The willingness to substitute Infinite Intelligence for our own intelligence, which society has grossly overrated, takes a lot of trust, faith and perseverance. Yet without that expression of trust, faith and perseverance we forego the opportunity to bring fulfillment into our lives through the ultimate experiences of peacefulness, aliveness, and joyfulness.

DEFINITION OF MASTERY

When have you achieved mastery of something? It is when you assume it works perfectly in your life. You release any concern or thought about it and release the need to influence or control it.

Take tennis as an example. The professionals who have mastered the game assume that they know how to hit the ball correctly, and just go ahead and hit it. Most people have achieved mastery of their experience with food. They assume that the body will do what is necessary to digest it. The average person does not worry about whether his glands will secrete the proper enzymes, or whether his blood will carry nutrients to the cells.

The same applies to our experience with money. We have mastered money when it is no longer a concern in our lives. We trust it to function perfectly. We go on with the rest of our lives, ideally, doing what we love and allowing the money to take care of itself. It does!

Remember, money is just a form of energy. If we wish it to flow freely in our lives, we must have no attachment to it and no concern about it. Thoughts of concern or attachment create energy blocks, and the flow is impeded. Trusting the Universe to provide us with what is best for us at all times will insure a free flow of money, and everything else.

THE PARADOX OF THE MATERIAL WORLD

Having a life of material abundance is simple, yet most people fail to achieve it. It is like trying to grasp a particle float-

117

ing in the air. When you try too hard, it eludes your grasp. As you move slowly, gently and lovingly it cooperates and allows you to have it.

The key to being in a relaxed, comfortable state that allows you to approach life in a gentle, loving manner is the *belief* that material abundance is your gift from the Universe. You need do only one thing to have it — play the real game. Whenever you focus on the spiritual aspect of life, the material aspect comes along as a gift. Going after material wealth directly will always be a struggle, and the cost will always exceed the benefit gained.

Question: You make it all sound so simple and easy.

Answer: It is. The Universe is an experience of ease and simplicity. One of the ways that you know you are dealing with the real Universe and the universal principles is when ideas and concepts are simple and easy. This is inherent in the concept of perfection. Remember, the Universe is by definition, perfect. When you notice that something is complicated, be suspicious. It is probably not in alignment with the Universe and Its principles.

It is now time for another break. Take a walk, listen to some music and do some exercise.

A dictionary definition of awareness, which is the next topic, is consciousness. It is a key to our progress in improving the quality of our lives. The opposite is unconsciousness, a word we apply to someone who is not alert to what is really going on.

Not only is it important that we are alert, but that we reach for a state of heightened awareness.

Let's start by taking a look at the concept.

AWARENESS

My observation is that most of us spend much of our time responding to descriptions of what is happening rather than to what is really happening. We believe we can comprehend everything that happens, so we reduce every experience to something we can describe. The description then becomes the substitute for the experience.

There is a simple way to find the meaning of life. Paradoxically, understanding comes only when we do not try to understand it. It is unfolded to us as we allow ourselves to be *aware* of our experiences without evaluating, analyzing or describing them.

Each of us has a built-in mechanism which is designed to guide us toward perfect responses to all events and experiences in our lives. I call this the PERFECT RESPONSE MECHANISM (PRM). It is the mechanism that is brilliant enough to digest food and take nutrients to the cells in order to support the life of the organism. It is the mechanism that enables a fielder to race to where a baseball will be hit, before he can have any conscious mind knowledge of where the ball is going. This mechanism can respond to an infinite number of stimuli instanteously and simultaneously, if we allow the stimuli to reach the mechanism unimpeded. Every time the conscious mind intervenes in any way to evaluate, analyze, or think about the stimulus, the PRM cannot do its job perfectly. It is akin to having a calculator available and doing all of our calculations without it.

To simplify the concept of the PRM, think of all of your sensory organs (eyes, ears, nose, skin and such) as located at one end of a tube. Picture a hinged flap across the middle of the inside of the tube. The flap represents your conscious mind. Visualize the PRM at the other end of the tube. Every time your conscious mind intervenes by evaluating, analyzing, describing, or judging any stimulus, you block the tube with the flap. This prevents the stimulus from passing through the tube to the PRM.

Whether we use it or not, the PRM is always available. As we use it, its brilliance is immediately evident. My suggestion is to use the PRM as often as possible. This requires us to keep our conscious minds from intervening.

Here are some simple exercises to help you to do this.

> Think of the places where you generally spend your time. Then create an awareness exercise that focuses the conscious mind on something in the immediate environment. Choose something which is appropriate to the environment and is interesting enough to keep the conscious mind engaged. For example, when driving your car, notice the energy changes that take place each time another vehicle passes by. Notice the difference in energy between a car passing in your direction and one going in the opposite direction. Notice the difference in energy between passing a car or a large truck, and passing parked cars or trees.

> When in your house or apartment select a dominant feature of each room and focus on that whenever you enter the room. For example, focus on odors when you go into your kitchen, or colors when you are in your living room. Focus on the texture or taste of each food while you are eating. It's fun to make up these exercises. Change them as often as is necessary to keep your conscious mind interested. As you lose interest, the conscious mind becomes free to roam around,

and it will often intervene between the stimuli and the PRM.

The beauty of these exercises is that the focus on *one* aspect of the immediate environment enhances the ability of the PRM to receive all other stimuli from that environment. The PRM not only responds perfectly to each stimulus, but its sequence of responses is also perfect.

Let's return to the example of the car. Focusing our conscious minds on the energy changes as we drive along, prevents us from evaluating the experience. (This keeps the flap in the tube in its open position and allows all of the stimuli in our immediate environment to pass directly from our sensory organs to the PRM.) Stimuli such as road noises, fumes, and tensions in our bodies are received by the PRM. The perfect response or sequence of responses is then transmitted to us, intuitively.

If we allow ourselves to evaluate the experience, we quickly find ourselves conceptualizing the situation. We think such thoughts as, "What an annoying trip this is," or "This highway is like a big parking lot." Once we conceptualize or judge the experience, we inhibit the natural operation of our PRM.

Our PRM is constantly leading us in the direction of a higher quality of life. It will create the circumstances to bring this about. For example, we become interested in finding a job with more convenient working hours or a more convenient location.

The PRM is never satisifed. It continually seeks a more perfect experience for us. Having improved our comfort, it will, if we allow it, improve the quality of the job.

PRM AND RELATIONSHIPS

Person to person interaction presents us with the most challenging context in which to use the PRM. This is because each of us is very good at convincing others that the way we present ourselves is the way we really are. We express anger, come late for appointments, act confused or show disrespect for others' feelings. This is just the closest we can come to expressing our real selves, at the time.

Strange as it may seem, anger is just a distorted expression of love. It is the nearest a person can come to expressing love, at that moment. When someone is able to see past the anger, and refuses to believe it, the angry person responds by releasing the anger.

So we come back once again to square one. Our experience of the world is determined by how we see it. When we practice seeing others as really loving us (in spite of how unloving their actions might be) we notice that our world changes to reflect our new perception of it.

The following awareness exercise illustrates how you can deal with an emotional illusion. Assume that you are experiencing what you perceive as anger toward another person.

Remind yourself that anger is an illusion.

Let go of the description of the experience you are having and just focus on the sensation in your body. The key element is breaking the connection between the sensation in your body and any thoughts attached to it. Once you release all of your thoughts about the sensation and focus only on it, the sensation will disappear.

The PRM is the active participant in the exercise. Remember the PRM always seeks to provide the perfect response to any situation, and to bring you back to your natural state of comfort. By eliminating your evaluation of the situation, you allow the stimulus to go unimpeded to the PRM which can then act appropriately.

If there is a strong connection between any of your thoughts and your feelings, it can take much repetition to break the connection. Continuing with the exercise will bring about changes in energy, and in the nature of the sensations in your body. As the connection is weakened, energy is released. When the connection is finally broken, you will respond spontaneously and freely to the person or event that created the discomfort in the first place.

Forgive the other person. Then forgive yourself.

Focus your attention on anything that induces a state of comfort and peacefulness. Do something you love to do.

Question: You stated that our PRM wants to lead us to a more perfect experience. You also stated that for us to improve the quality of our lives, we must actively focus on doing so. There seems to be an inconsistency between the two thoughts.

Answer: That is a perceptive comment and I'll enjoy answering it. The PRM is really the part of each of us that is connected to Infinite Intelligence. That is how it knows how to respond perfectly to every situation. If we had no preconceived ideas and beliefs as to how the world worked, and just allowed the Universe to guide us, we would continually experience perfection. What stands in the way then, are our beliefs and our vested interests in having things a certain way.

The exercises suggested in this chapter are simple ways of allowing our natural response mechanism, the PRM, to function.

The process is completed when we change all beliefs that bring us discomfort. However, while we are in the process of changing our beliefs, it is helpful to bypass them as often as possible. This helps us to reach those states of comfort and happiness that life is really all about.

The more we can experience *being* there, the greater our incentive to release all beliefs that keep us from *staying* there.

OUR RELATIONSHIP WITH OUR SOURCE

Do you believe that God or an Infinite Intelligence is responsible for human life and everything else in the Universe? If the answer is yes, do you see It as an unconditionally loving and supportive energy? It is interesting that the way you view the energy, is exactly the way that you will experience life. If you can bring yourself to honestly and completely believe that It is totally loving, and supportive of everyone, under all circumstances, then you will experience a life of total joy. The degree that your belief is less than that, is the degree to which your life experience will be less than totally joyful.

There are people who believe that it is better to focus on a concept other than God to explain the creation of the Universe. When this is an attempt to avoid the concept of God, because thoughts related to God are unpleasant, then the replacement will not work.

As long as you harbor any thoughts that God is less than a totally loving and supportive entity, these thoughts will block you from achieving the peace of mind and joy that you wish to achieve.

When we view God as less than a totally loving and supportive entity, we view people as less than totally loving and supportive. Those of us who can see the perfection and unconditional love of God can see the same quality in others and in the Universe.

In our relationship with our Universe and with other people, we are truly experiencing the mirror image of our beliefs. It is a very simple, but powerful concept. The best investment we can ever make is to learn to see everything and everyone around us as perfect. For then, we see ourselves that way, and we actually experience life that way.

GOD IS OUR FRIEND

Viewed another way, God is not a separate entity, but a unified wholistic, energy that encompasses everything and everyone in the Universe. In truth, *we are all one*. When we believe this, it becomes our experience and we have achieved a major breakthrough.

We can be certain to feel joy when we are giving or receiving unconditional love and support, and this will never change. It is a part of the human condition, and the solution to all of our problems. In our consciousness, God represents everyone and everything. When God becomes our friend, so will everyone else.

THE GAME OF LIFE AND HOW TO WIN IT

To win any game requires a clear understanding of the rules. It also requires a clear *intention* to win. The game of life has the same requirement as any other game. Preparing to play soccer by buying a rule book on baseball is not helpful. The reason many people do not enjoy a high quality life is that they are not certain which is the real game and have not mastered the rules.

This book has described the real game and outlined and explained the rules for you. Once you agree with the rules and have chosen to play the game, the results you achieve are then dependent on your *intention to succeed*. Surprising as it may seem, if your *intention is to succeed* in the new game immediately, you will achieve that result. (Remember the law of cause and effect.) Winning the game right from the start is possible because the Universe will acknowledge your *intention* immediately, and will give you such generous support that the quality of your life will improve dramatically, and will continue to improve with each step you take.

There is no end to improving the quality of your life. No matter how wonderful it might seem at any level you have achieved, the possibility of improvement always exists, and the game never ends.

Playing the real game is fun wherever and whenever you do it. It is as much fun for a beginner as for an advanced player. Think of any activity you love to participate in. The level of skill is not as important as the joy of participation. A child who loves to play baseball receives as much pleasure playing on a sand lot as a superstar does playing in a major league stadium.

Start playing the real game right away and allow yourself the pleasure and enjoyment that comes from playing the one game that each of us has the talent to win every moment we play. It's a sure bet. Just listen to your intuition. Our Coach never gave a wrong signal and never lost a game.

———————————

The next concept is one that explains what we can expect when we shift from one career focus to another.

OWNING THE LEVEL

Once we have achieved mastery of anything in our lives, we own the level attained by that achievement. What's more, the skills used to attain that level are transferable. We see illustrations of this principle all of the time.

Look at the business section of your newspaper and you will often see that a president of a major corporation has transferred to another major corporation whose product or service is totally different from the one he left. Once a person functions at a presidential level, he owns that level and moves around in society at that level.

Society places different values on talents. A person who is talented in business or in the professions is accorded a higher status than one whose talent is in sewing, cooking, repairing appliances, or hanging wallpaper. Yet, *each talent is truly equal in value to every other talent*.

It is important that we support ourselves and others in this thought. As our perception of the value of our talent improves, so will the actual value, to us and to others. The person who sews, knits, or cooks, with great skill, is entitled to the same acknowledgment as the successful president of a major corporation. Each is entitled to be treated as a superstar. However, *others always treat us in the ways we wish to be treated. Until we view what we do as important and valuable, no one else will*.

In our area of talent, we are all potential superstars. Since, along with every talent comes the tools to express it perfectly, we can become superstars when we are ready. Others will view us as superstars when we view ourselves that way.

Question: Are you saying that once we have achieved a high level of success at any one thing, we then function at that level in whatever we pursue?

Answer: That is exactly what I am saying. Many people express their talents at very high levels of performance and yet they do not acknowledge themselves for what they have accomplished. This is often the case with those who express their talents as avocations, such as sewing or knitting exquisitely, or repairing gadgets miraculously.

Each of us was given one or more talents. When we are in touch with our real selves through the full and free expression of our talents, our whole life experience is different. The perfection of the Universe is such, that it is intended for our lives to work perfectly, with ease and simplicity. It is only when we lead from our talents that it all comes together.

Another way of viewing it is to recognize that each of us is a genius when it comes to expressing our personal talent or talents. Why not allow ourselves to be the geniuses we truly are, and receive all the joy that expressing as a genius allows?

On a practical level this means that when our career focus and talents merge, we can expect to succeed quickly. We can reach a level of success that is equivalent to the greatest success we have enjoyed to date. In fact, we can expect to go to a much higher level. For the Universe will exhibit Its support in recognition and response to our alignment with It and Its purpose.

INSIDE OUT

Changing the world around us really doesn't ever give us more than temporary pleasure. Changing the world around us is exhausting. Most of us spend our entire lives changing things in our environment in an effort to improve the quality of our lives. We seek more money, newer and fancier cars, more expensive houses, and more beautiful clothes as ways to feel better.

The pleasure brought by this approach is only short-lived. It cannot last, since it results from an illusory belief, which is contrary to our reason for being. We are not here to accumulate things or to amass wealth.

The Universe created us to express ourselves as perfect reflections of Itself. We are the vehicles of the Universe. We serve one another by giving freely of our talents and rendering services or making products which we create by virtue of these talents. The natural result of this process is that money and other material wealth flows easily throughout our lives.

Whenever we reverse this process and make money the primary motivating factor, we lose. Seeking money, or other material things, invariably puts us in a position where we fail to support other people as our first priority. The Universe never misses an opportunity to remind us of our priorities. The reminder comes in the form of a feeling of discomfort. The irony is that we can have all the things we require to enjoy a life that works perfectly, provided we change our priorities.

Your first priority is to master the basic laws of the Universe. This will create the inner changes that will attract more abundance than you ever dreamed possible. As you trust the Universe, you will find that abundance is your natural state of being, and that perfect things will flow into your life, just as you need them.

CRITERIA AND STANDARDS

What are your criteria for a successful life? The human being is so created that she requires one or more standards or criteria to form the guidelines for her life experience. The society in which we live encourages us to adopt material wealth, status, physical beauty and competitiveness as our standards. Since society introduces these criteria to us in our formative years, we tend to adopt them without being conscious of the impact they have on our lives. They become our standards, on a subconscious level, governing our lives though we often have no awareness of them.

When we adopt these criteria, they become our beliefs. Beliefs, as we know, operate as the causative element, under the law of cause and effect. Another way of saying this is that they become our wants. Since we always receive what we want, our lives assume whatever shape is fashioned by these criteria.

Fortunately, the Universe is not a passive bystander. Its standard for Itself, and for us, is perfection. While It gives each of us the choice to adopt whatever standards we wish, It also establishes the *consequences* for the choices we make. The Universe truly wants us to experience a life that works perfectly and so It continues to signal us everytime we make a choice.

We were each created for a purpose. That purpose is not to accumulate wealth, achieve status, and compete with one another. Selection of criteria such as these invariably result in experiences of discomfort, as the Universe never misses an opportunity to encourage us to align with It in purpose.

There is a simple solution to this apparent problem and that is to adopt different criteria for our lives. By selecting criteria such as perfection, peace, joy, serenity and love (each one being an aspect of the other) we place ourselves in alignment with the Universe and open ourselves to Its abundant support. Once we adopt any one of these criteria, we reap the benefits of all other aspects which align with it. In other words, we guarantee that *we have it all*.

Built into the human species is the need to give and receive unconditional love. It is something that is an integral part of us. Whenever we look for it, we find it, and whenever we express it, we immediately receive all of the benefits of being in perfect alignment with the Universe.

Seeing the perfection in ourselves and everyone around us, or at least making that our goal, is an ideal criterion. It is a continual reminder of who we really are. It guarantees us the support of the Universe, as we move toward having a life that works perfectly.

Question: I seem to be following what you are saying and yet it appears too simple. Do I understand that all we have to do is focus all of our attention on perfection and everything else will be taken care of?

Answer: Yes. That is the beauty and the simplicity of dealing with the highest thoughts. Remember, the Universe already functions perfectly. We, as a product of that perfect Universe are created to function perfectly. Believing this is a choice we make. The Universe continually provides signals as to how we can move into alignment with It, but it will not make the choice for us. As soon as we realize that the real game allows all of us to be winners, and that in fact the Universe guarantees it, the only decision left is whether or not to play the real game.

We do not have to do anything to make ourselves perfect — we already are perfect. Our life experience is the opportunity to release all beliefs that we are less than perfect, right now.

The more we allow ourselves to believe in our perfection, the more we open ourselves to the abundance of the Universe. It wants to flow through our lives. It is we who either keep it out, or let it in.

HOW TO CHANGE WHAT WE WANT

The law of cause and effect tells us that we always receive what we want. When we notice we are receiving results that are unsatisfactory, we must change what it is that we presently want, in order to change the results.

The first step in changing what you want is to truly recognize that what you now have is what you want, even though you think you want something else.

The second step is to recognize that anything that is less than perfect is an illusion. Thus what you are about to release is an illusion. Taking note of this will weaken your attachment to it.

Illusions only remain in existence as long as you put energy into them. The way you do this is by talking or thinking about them. To rid yourself of an illusion requires that you make believe it does not exist, and go to a higher thought. The most appropriate higher thought is one that is either a basic principle or a thought that is in alignment with a basic principle. Whenever the illusion returns, you repeat the procedure until it is finally released.

The third step is to remind yourself that nothing is right or wrong, good or bad.

The fourth step is to recognize that you must select the replacement for what you wanted. Nature abhors a vacuum. Thus it is difficult to relieve yourself of what you are dissatisfied with, unless you replace it with something else.

The fifth step is to remember that the Universe handles the details. So when creating the replacement, do not focus on details.

The final step is to create in your mind the most ideal quality of life experience you can think of. Let go of any preconceived ideas. Allow your creative mind to soar and become joyous. Think of the most wonderful way you can *feel*. Do this every day. Each successive day, make the quality of the experience more wonderful and more joyful. Keep stretching yourself until you are totally satisfied that you have reached a perfect state.

EXAMPLE

Assume the result you are now experiencing is a cashflow shortage, more debts than income.

> Be in touch with the fact that you want to be in debt, precisely as you are, with these exact creditors and exactly this amount of debt.
>
> Recognize that a shortage of cash flow is an illusion. In experiencing shortage, you are *creating* it by resisting the natural flow of abundance in your life. Then practice feeling comfortable about benefitting your debtors. Do it separately with each one.[28]

Remind yourself that the creation of the debt is not something bad that you have done, and the creditor is not wrong for asking for payment.

Select the *new* want. For example, choose an abundance of cash flow with perfect balance between income and expenses.

Let the Universe handle the details.

Define a day of abundance. Notice all the abundance you presently have. Acknowledge and give thanks for each experience of abundance you have. Then notice the feeling quality of a perfectly abundant day.[29] Keep focusing on the ideal. That puts energy into it.

In summary, we must always be sensitive to what we want in the present moment. By noticing what we are receiving, we know what that is. Changing what we want requires a clear and definite *intention* to change it, as well as a clear idea of what we wish to have in its place.

NOTE

It is important to bear in mind that in order to bring about change in our lives, we must have a one hundred percent intention to create a change. Anything less than one hundred percent equals zero percent. The way we know that the intention has reached one hundred percent is when the change occurs. Until the change actually occurs, we know we do not yet really wish to change.

Mastery of the principles requires us to tell the truth at all times, particularly to ourselves. (We will not tell the truth to others if we do not tell the truth to ourselves.)

We do not bring about change by just making an intellectual decision. The change occurs when we truly *want* it.

MEANS AND ENDS

There is only one way to achieve any goal that you set for yourself.

> To achieve inner peace, you think inner peace and act peacefully, moment by moment.
>
> To achieve unconditional love, you think unconditional love and act unconditionally loving, moment by moment.
>
> To achieve a life that works perfectly, you think perfection and see the perfection in yourself and everyone else, moment by moment.
>
> To experience total abundance in your life, you think and feel the abundance all around you, moment by moment.
>
> The principle is simple. Means and ends are always identical.

RELEASING PROBLEMS

The major obstacle to resolving problems in our lives is that we deal with them as though they are something outside of us. The truth is that every problem is an outward manifestation of our state of consciousness. When our consciousness is clear and at peace, the problem disappears.

Every attempt we make to resolve a problem by changing something outside of ourselves will be unsuccessful. It might temporarily ease the situation, but the problem will not be released permanently until there is a change of consciousness.

An example illustrates the principle involved. Assume you owe someone $1000.00. She is demanding payment and you have only $100.00 cash on hand. Attempts to raise $900.00 by borrowing or working overtime can temporarily resolve the problem. Looking at it from a higher perspective, you recognize that you created the debt and the lack of funds to repay it on time. Understanding that you want the problem and the accompanying discomfort is the first step in its permanent resolution. Also, realizing that you want to withhold money from the creditor is an essential next step. The final clearing of your consciousness comes when you can feel the desire to freely and happily benefit the creditor. Once this occurs, the funds to do it will appear or the creditor may forgive the debt.

Remember, the world of illusion teaches us about the state of *our* consciousness. We literally create all of our problems and they do not disappear until we clear our consciousness of the issue represented by the problem.

What we consider our toughest problems are just reflections of those issues which we have the most resistance to resolving. Another way of stating it is that we would rather experience discomfort by continuing with the problem, than releasing the discomfort by allowing ourselves to express love to another person. Ultimately, we recognize that other person is us.

WAYS TO GENERATE MORE ABUNDANCE

ACKNOWLEDGE ALL OF THE ABUNDANCE YOU ALREADY HAVE

Give thanks for your friends and family. Give thanks for the trees, sun, beaches, rivers, mountains, and birds. Give thanks for the food you eat, the clothes you wear, your house or apartment, your car, the money in your pocket and in the bank. This is a wonderful exercise. It is so simple and it is so powerful. There is a basic principle operating each time you do this. The principle is: *whatever you focus your thoughts on expands.* The more you notice and acknowledge all of the things that you have, the more you will receive.

The converse is also true. If you dwell upon what you do not have, you put energy into scarcity and you will experience more of it. This is a simple principle and one well worth mastering. Remember, anything less than perfection is an illusion. Scarcity is an illusion. The natural state of the Universe is abundance. *When you are not experiencing abundance you are pushing it away from yourself.* As you practice acknowledging and giving thanks for all that you have, you will break up the old pattern and replace it with one that puts you in alignment with the abundance of the Universe.

SPEND MORE TIME DOING WHAT YOU LOVE

Doing what you love is an expression of your talent. Your talent and creativity are two gifts which have been given to you as an expression of the abundance of the Universe. When used in conjunction with each other, there is no limit to the further abundance you can create for yourself.

KEEP YOUR IDEAL DAY IN MIND

This is a wonderful way to express your joyfulness and attract the people and circumstances that will bring abundance into your life.

PARTICIPATE IN A SUPPORT SYSTEM

This puts you into interaction with others who love and support you unconditionally. It is the best environment for you to change your patterns, avoid falling back into old patterns and practice the basic principles. The more ways you can create and give yourself support for using the basic principles, the easier it will become and the faster you will achieve mastery.

Remember, you can not give to others what you have not allowed yourself to receive. So be good and kind to yourself. You deserve it. Then give freely to others, as you allow others to continue to give freely to you.

NOTICE WHAT WORKS FOR YOU AND CONTINUE DOING IT

Forget about why things are the way they

are. This is irrelevant. Just notice how they are now. When you notice something that makes you feel comfortable, enjoy it and do it often. Be careful not to misinterpret this. I am referring to a deep feeling of satisfaction and peacefulness that encompasses you and those around you.

MEDITATION

One of the best ways to learn to distinguish between what is real and what is an illusion is through the practice of meditation. This is quiet time devoted to contemplating our real selves and our relationship to God.

We can not spend too much time reminding ourselves of this relationship. This is also the time when we remind ourselves that our spiritual being is our real self, and that It is connected to all other beings.

Finally, meditation provides an opportunity to be in touch with the motivating factor, the life force behind the infinite supply of energy in the Universe; that which connects and supports all of us is *love*.

One of the benefits of meditation is that it helps us to achieve a state of relaxation. It is only when we are relaxed that we can be truly creative. We allow ourselves to relax when we believe that whatever is perfect for us is a gift from the Universe, awaiting our readiness to receive it.

Fear, anxiety or any other emotional state is simply the result of our withholding love from ourselves and others. When we are in such an emotional state, we create the tension that precludes feeling love.

Our major misperception is the belief that the world, as we experience it, is real. When we meditate, we remind ourselves to align with the Universe and allow Its perfection to flow through us as the source of our creativity and our sustenance.

SAFETY

There is total safety in the Universe at all times. We do not have to do anything to save ourselves or the Universe. Acting out of a sense of urgency does not lead to high quality performance. As we feel the peace of the Universe, we can express fully and freely who we really are in ways that truly support the perfection of the Universe.

The only way we can feel the total safety of the Universe is when we are unconditionally loving and supporting another person, or receiving unconditional love and support. This is when we are in touch with what is real in us and others, and with the Universe.

Our essence, and the essence of everything else in the Universe cannot die. Until we believe that, our life experience is one of continual fear of death. Our essence can not experience anything but joyfulness. Until we believe that, we live in continual fear that something bad, terrible, or painful can happen to us at any time.

Our essence cannot experience pain or death. Since we have the capacity to express from our essence who we really are, we have the ability to live a life of joy, forever. The choice is always ours.

Remember, when you are ready, YOU CAN HAVE IT ALL.

SUPPORT

The Universe functions as a *mutual support system*. Everything in the Universe relates to everything else. The sun provides the energy for growth of plants which in turn provide food for animals. The planets exert gravitational influences on each other. Our use of the resources on our planet influences the quality of the air we breathe and the water we drink. Since every thought has some impact on the physical universe, each of us is continually influencing the quality of our environment. We are part of a mutual support system.

Our ability to function successfully within a mutual support system is related to our willingness to recognize and believe that this is indeed the nature of our life experience. Society tends to teach us differently. It encourages us to strike out on our own and work to achieve personal objectives and goals. We are left with the impression that we can achieve happiness at the expense of others, or at least without caring about others.

It is important then, to keep reminding ourselves that the Universe creates us to function in the context of a mutual support system. Unless we are ever mindful of the interrelatedness of each and every person and thing in the Universe, we cannot enjoy the benefit of the perfect design of the universal system.

The basic laws of the Universe are the guidelines for life within this mutual support system. Following them places us in alignment with every one and every thing within the system.

We see this mutual support system functioning, to varying degrees, within families, clubs, associations, religious organizations and businesses.

When we operate within the world of illusion, we often establish rules and standards for groups which are not in alignment with the basic laws of the Universe. Therefore, as you may have noticed, many groups do not provide an ideal level of support for their members.

It is possible for people everywhere to create support groups for themselves. These six simple guidelines will enable a group of people (a group is two or more people) to act as a mutual support group.

SEE THE PERFECTION IN EVERYTHING

This is a reminder that we experience everything the way we perceive it. There is no event that is good or bad, right or wrong.[30] Consider once again the example of the cut finger. You can become angry at yourself for causing yourself pain. Or you can be thankful that the Universe, through the pain, is reminding you of a self-destructive tendency which you can release and replace with behavior that is self-supportive and pleasurable, now that it is brought to your attention.

STATE EVERYTHING IN PRESENT TIME

The only time that ever exists is the present moment. (The past is gone forever and the future is yet to be.) The ideal is for each of us to be so completely in the present moment that we are at one with it, disregarding everything that is not a part of it. As we learn to trust the Universe more, we allow ourselves to focus more in the present moment and have it be a more perfect experience. By stating our thoughts in the present tense, we are continually reminding ourselves of this principle.

EVERYONE SUPPORTS EVERYONE ELSE

This is a reminder that we are part of a mutual support system. We are all dependent upon one another. As we support each other, we support ourselves.

ACT AS THOUGH YOU ARE NOW LIVING YOUR LIFE AS YOU IDEALLY LIKE IT TO BE

The only way to improve your life is to conceive of a better one.[31] Once you conceive of it, then make believe it is real. If you practice having a better life, it will help you believe it can be that way.

Remember however, that the Universe handles the details.[32] When conceiving of a better life, focus on the way you *wish to feel*. Locate the inner joyfulness. Open yourself to it, and allow it to expand so that it fills you with its warmth and happiness. This is your real self. Cultivate it, nurture it, and it will grow to fill your life with its presence.

As you express joy, you draw it out of those you meet, creating joyful people and joyful events. The greater the joy you express, the more joy you experience, until eventually, you realize that only joy is real. All else is illusion. How do you feel right now?

EVERYONE GENTLY, KINDLY AND LOVINGLY REMINDS EVERYONE ELSE OF THE GUIDELINES WHEN THEY ARE NOT BEING OBSERVED

It is the responsibility of each member of the

group to keep the group on purpose. This is done in a gentle, kind and loving manner. Any story can be told, any event recounted or any problem presented in a way that is in alignment with the principles discussed in this book. It helps everyone to guide the presenter toward an approach that supports him and the others in the group.

EVERYONE HAS AN OPPORTUNITY TO COMPLETE

In order to remove time as an issue, each member of a group remains available, whenever asked, to support the other members. This removes the pressure of having to deal with something at a time when a member is not ready.

The foregoing guidelines served to launch the support system. However, additional guidelines were needed to maintain the focus and positive energy of a group whenever a participant presented a personal problem.

THE ELEVEN STEPS is just such a guideline. It contains a series of suggestions and questions that enables the presenter to perceive the problem in the context of universal principles.

To increase the effectiveness of the procedure, the other participants remain silent while the presenter speaks. However, it is an active silence with each person focusing attention and support on the presenter. (The specific guidelines for this are offered on page 87 where instructions for the INTUITIVE DIALOGUE are given.) The major function of the listener is to provide so much love and support for the presenter, that he feels free to say what is true for him, at that moment. The insights gained by the presenter during this experience prove invaluable in assisting with the resolution of the problem.

There is another way that the INTUITIVE DIALOGUE can be used. The leader suggests a topic that every person in the group meditates on at the same time. An example of such a topic is: The truth for me about what I love to do is.....
Everyone meditates on this thought until the first person is ready to speak. After the first person is finished speaking, the next person then speaks. This continues until everyone who wishes to express his response to the meditation does so. A participant may speak more than once.

THE ELEVEN STEPS
(PROCEDURE TO RE-PERCEIVE A PROBLEM)

When a participant presents to the group a situation that is causing him discomfort, the following step-by-step procedure is suggested. A member of the group reads the following instructions, one at a time, allowing the person with the situation to respond to each instruction before proceeding to the next one.

DEFINE THE SITUATION.

This step is to allow the person to explain, as briefly as possible, what is causing the discomfort. Once the situation has been defined, the exercise can begin.

CLOSE YOUR EYES AND BECOME AWARE OF THE FEELING IN YOUR BODY, SEPARATE FROM ANY THOUGHTS YOU MAY HAVE ABOUT IT. INDICATE WHEN THE DISCOMFORT LEAVES.

The reason for this step is to help the person separate the feelings in his body from all thoughts he may have about them. The chapter on emotion explains the importance of this.[33] As long as a thought is attached to a feeling, discomfort is experienced in our bodies.

ARE YOU WILLING TO TAKE TOTAL RESPONSIBILITY FOR ALL ASPECTS OF THE SITUATION? IN WHAT WAY?

This question is a reminder of the law of cause and effect.

DO YOU AGREE THAT NOTHING YOU OR ANYONE ELSE HAS DONE OR IS DOING IS EITHER WRONG OR RIGHT? PLEASE EXPLAIN.

This question reminds the presenter that as long as he is judging himself or anyone else, he will be locked in the discomfort he is presently experiencing. The only way to release the discomfort is to release all judgment of everyone and everything including himself.

PERCEIVE THE SITUATION DIFFERENTLY. CREATE ANOTHER INTERPRETATION OF IT.

Everything we experience is a result of our perception of it. When our perception changes, the experience changes. In order for a person to perceive a troubling situation in a different way, he must let go of his attachment to his present perception of the situation. It is his unwillingness to do this that is a major cause of the situation in the first place. After a couple of minutes of meditation, if the presenter is unable to perceive the situation differently, he is told to continue meditating on this step at home, until he is successful in perceiving it differently.

My experience has taught me that while suggestions from others in the group as to how the presenter can perceive the situation differently may appear to benefit the presenter, in the long run only the presenter's self-initiated change in perception of the situation is of lasting benefit.

DO YOU REALIZE THAT YOU ARE RECEIVING EXACTLY WHAT YOU WANT AND THE OTHER PERSON(S) IS RECEIVING EXACTLY WHAT HE WANTS? PLEASE EXPLAIN.

This is another reminder of the law of cause and effect.

DO YOU RECOGNIZE THAT THE WAY YOU SEE THE OTHER PERSON IS REALLY THE WAY YOU SEE YOURSELF? DO YOU WISH TO SHARE AN EXAMPLE?

DO YOU REALIZE THAT WHAT YOU ARE EXPERIENCING IS PRECISELY HOW YOU SEE THE SITUATION?

These are reminders that the way you see others or situations is a reflection of your state of consciousness. It is the most efficient way to find out what you really believe.

PLEASE DESCRIBE THE WAYS YOU ARE WITHHOLDING LOVE FROM YOURSELF AND OTHERS.

All discomfort involves a withholding of love. Locating the withholding helps to clarify what is really going on.

GO BEHIND THE APPARENT CIRCUMSTANCES OF THE SITUATION AND LOCATE THE LOVE IN YOURSELF AND IN ALL OTHERS INVOLVED IN THE SITUATION.

This is a reminder that the only true motivation for all behavior is love. When anyone's behavior is less than loving, it is just the closest that the person can come at that moment to expressing love.

FEEL THE JOY THAT COMES WHEN THE LOVE IS FOUND AND EXPRESSED.

This puts a person in touch with what is always there, if he looks for it.

The foregoing guidelines are designed to keep the participants of a support group in alignment with the basic principles of the Universe. A support group can function as an ideal family, giving each participant the opportunity to practice the principles in a safe, supportive environment. As each participant learns that life outside the support group is no different from life inside, he experiments with the use of the principles in all settings of his life. Many participants in existing support groups have successfully transferred their mastery of the principles to their lives outside the support groups, thereby allowing their whole world to be a support system. Remember, *we experience life the way we perceive it.*

When using THE ELEVEN STEPS, one of the participants in the group acts as the leader and guides the person with the situation through the procedure. Ideally, the process is done using the INTUITIVE DIALOGUE.³⁴ approach. INTUITIVE DIALOGUE is a technique that allows the presenter to speak honestly about what is on his mind, after meditating on each step. The group listens attentively, making no response. This way the presenter learns what he really believes about the issues raised by each step in the process.

Learning the truth about our beliefs is the first step in changing them. Once we know what they are, we can begin to take responsibility for them. Once we truly understand that we have created our beliefs in the first place, we know that only we have the power to change them.

GUIDELINES FOR
THE INTUITIVE DIALOGUE

WHEN SPEAKING

Present whatever comes up for you — an idea, a concern, an experience, anything.

Speak clearly and audibly.

Be open, honest and direct without hurting anyone.

Give only as much explanation as is necessary for others to understand you fully.

SPEAK WITHOUT

Stating agreement or disagreement.

Judging or blaming yourself or another.

Defending your position or self-image.

Avoiding or skirting the real issue.

WHEN LISTENING

Give the speaker your full attention.

If a distraction arises, lay it aside without judgment and listen again.

Honor the speaker's willingness to present what is true for him.

LISTEN WITHOUT

Responding, even non verbally (smiling, frowning or nodding).

Agreeing, disagreeing, evaluating or judging.

Imposing your own attitudes and beliefs.

Rehearsing what you will say when it is your turn.

Talking to another listener during the dialogue.

Leaving the group while another is speaking.

SUGGESTED OUTLINE FOR A TYPICAL SUPPORT GROUP MEETING

START ON TIME.

SELECT A LEADER FOR THE MEETING.

Alternate leaders at subsequent meetings. Choose, as leader, a person who is feeling happy and is eager to support others.

CENTER THE ENERGY IN THE GROUP.

Sit in a circle and have the leader focus everyone's attention on a thought such as, "We are all grateful for the opportunity to be together and to offer our love and support to each other."

THE ELEVEN STEPS.

Each person announces a number between one and ten. A high number indicates that it is important to the person that he have the opportunity to go through the ELEVEN STEPS at the meeting. More than one person can announce the same number.

The leader takes each participant (high numbers first) who wishes to do so, through the ELEVEN STEPS.

The participant (now the presenter) is free to stop the exercise at any time. It is always his choice, as the group is there to support the presenter.

It is important to remember that no participant is to suggest a solution to a presenter, either during or after the exercise. The ELEVEN STEPS is the sole method used to deal with the situation being presented. Solutions suggested by others are not helpful. Meaningful change occurs for the presenter when he gains his own insight as to the solution of his situation.

Feeling the unconditional love and support of the group provides the presenter with the environment of safety that encourages him to tell the truth to himself. Each member allows whatever the presenter says to be perfect, whether or not he agrees with the statement. This enables the group to feel what unconditional love and support is like.

If the presenter has any difficulty with Step #5 (Perceive The Situation Differently) of the ELEVEN STEPS, the leader suggests that the presenter continue with Step #5 at home. The exercise is then continued by proceeding to the next step.

EACH PARTICIPANT READS HIS INDIVIDUAL PRUPOSE.

The group members feel the statement with the presenter as it is read.

READ THE GROUP PURPOSE.

To arrive at the group purpose, each member, on his own, defines his purpose for the group. Each member then reads his statement of purpose for the group which then arrives at a single statement of group purpose.

It is important that the statement reflect the group's purpose on a feeling level. The participants hold hands as they read the statement aloud together. Modifications are suggested until every member feels inspired when the statement is read.

The group purpose is read and felt by the entire group at every meeting. Whenever the purpose ceases to feel inspiring, it is time to modify it.

IDEAL FEELING.

Each person, in turn, closes her eyes and scans her body, noticing how she feels. Feeling fine, she enjoys and expands this wonderful feeling. However, if any feeling of discomfort is noticed, she relaxes into it until it is released. The person then expands the feeling of relaxation into a feeling of joyfulness, remaining there for a few moments. When complete, she opens her eyes and the next person begins. After all participants are complete, they hold hands and feel their ideal feelings together.

REVIEW A PRINCIPLE.

REQUESTS FOR SPECIFIC SUPPORT.

Each person makes a request for specific support. Remember that all improvement in the quality of one's life begins in consciousness. The request for support focuses on support in consciousness. For example, a person is having difficulty in forgiving a friend. The request to the group is for support in feeling forgiveness for the friend and for herself. Once a person is able to make a clear request for support in consciousness, success is guaranteed. The only variable is the willingness of the person requesting the support to sustain the clear intention to achieve the desired result. Asking for the support strengthens the commitment to oneself.

Another example is of a person experiencing a shortage of cash flow. That person may request support for repeating the definition of abundance in front of the mirror until he feels the abundance of the Universe at a deep feeling level; and for continually acknowledging all of the abundance he presently has.

After the request for specific support is stated, the group responds to the member, "_____, we unconditionally love and support you just the way you are in all your magnificence."

EACH PERSON STATES WAYS IN WHICH USE OF THE PRINCIPLES HAS BEEN HELPFUL OR BENEFICIAL AND WAYS IN WHICH REQUESTS FOR SUPPORT HAVE BEEN HELPFUL.

THE POSITIVE REFLECTION EXERCISE.

In this exercise, group members see positive qualities in each of the other members of the group, which are reflected in themselves.

For example: In looking at one person you realize she has qualities of gentleness and kindness. In looking at another person you immediately feel his humor and joyfulness.

The exercise is carried out in this manner:

> Each participant receives a description of his positive qualities from every member of the group in turn. Then the next person in the group becomes the recipient.
>
> The person speaking looks directly into the eyes of the recipient and says, "Positive qualities I see in you, that you reflect for me are: _____."

The recipient responds by saying, "Thank you."

The exercise continues until every group member has had a chance to receive acknowledgments.

This exercise demonstrates the principle behind giving and receiving. When a person gives acknowledgment to another, he is really acknowledging himself. It is a simultaneous gift from the giver to another and from the giver to himself. This is a very powerful exercise. As the group bonds and the members deepen their appreciation for each other, the exercise serves to anchor and expand the depth of their feelings.

This exercise may be done periodically or upon request.

ENGAGE IN A FUN ACTIVITY SUCH AS GROUP SINGING OR A GROUP GAME.

SET THE DATE AND TIME FOR THE NEXT MEETING.

END THE MEETING ON TIME.

GROUP PURPOSE AND ALIGNMENT

We have previously discussed individual purpose,[35] and group purpose, as it applies to support groups.[36] The concept of group purpose is so helpful that I wish to address its application to all other group experiences.

When two or more people (group) come together for reasons that are social, personal, business, or anything which is more than casual, it is essential for them to focus on their purpose for being together. This becomes the group purpose. In the same way that a person's individual purpose creates the inspiration for her life, the group purpose creates the inspiration for the life of the group.

When there is clear alignment in purpose amongst the participants, each moves forward in the activities of the group with total confidence and certainty of success. It is well worth the time it takes to define the group purpose and clarify alignments with it before proceeding with the formalization of the group.

A simple way to define the group purpose is for each participant in the group to separately define the purpose for the group. Then the participants share their purposes with each other. Next, the group creates a single statement of group purpose. This is done with everyone's participation, at a group meeting. There is no need to rush the completion of the statement. However, it is important that the definition of group purpose be a priority agenda item at each meeting until it is completed.

There is no other factor that is of more value to the participants than a clearly defined group purpose, that inspires every member of the group. In fact, without such a purpose, there is little reason for the group to continue. The definition of the group purpose assures the success of the group. This is so important to understand that it is fair to say that the most important thing any group ever does is to define and redefine its purpose. It is the understanding of and alignment with purpose that accomplishes everything.

Remember, we live our lives at the consciousness level. Defining purpose in universal terms is aligning with the power of the Universe. It is the Universe working through us that creates ideal results. Our sole function is to keep ourselves in alignment with the Universe. When a group aligns with the Universe the power expressed through the group is expanded enormously. Every member of the group not only feels that power but enjoys the confidence and certainty that it represents.

The foregoing recommendations apply to a group that is about to form. Existing groups are approached in an entirely different way.

When a person is in an existing group, be it a marriage, social club, business venture, or any other kind, it is most helpful to look at the group in terms of the THREE STEP.[37]

First, recognize that you are in the situation because you created it. If the situation is less than ideal, remind yourself that your experience with the group reflects the present state of your consciousness.

Second, don't judge yourself or others in the group. This locks the energy within you. If you notice any judgment on your part, it is helpful to practice forgiving all those whom you are judging. Continue the practice daily until all judgment is released. Then shift the focus to feeling unconditional love for the other group member(s). Remember, whenever we judge another, we are really judging a part of ourselves. When we finally feel unconditional love for the other person, we come to love a part of ourselves from which we previously withheld love.

Third, ask yourself how you would ideally like to feel in connection with the group experience. Remember, if you wish to improve the quality of your life, you must first be willing to conceive of it being better than it presently is and then feel what that is like. This leads you to the IDEAL DAY EXERCISE.[38]

Doing the THREE STEP in connection with existing relationships enables us to come to peace with these relationships. It is only when we are at peace that forward movement occurs.

Assume the existing group experience is a job that we presently perceive as less than ideal. Following the foregoing procedure will lead to one of two probable outcomes: Either we find that having come to peace with the people involved, the job is now wonderful, or we are led to another job.

Every group has the potential to be an ideal support group. Even if you are the only one in the group who is willing to see the others as perfect just the way they are, that willingness on your part is sufficient to change the feeling quality of the group in a very significant way. Others will change in response to your change.

Our alignments with others reflect our alignment with the Universe. Time is not an issue. It is helpful to be patient and allow as long as it takes to bring ourselves into alignment with others. However, it is important to focus on alignment continually. This sustains the forward movement. Remember, this is all done at the consciousness level. As changes occur at this level, they are reflected in our daily experiences.

One of the greatest tools for improving our alignments is the definition of group purpose. Whenever there is apparent lack of alignment, it means either that the group purpose is not being defined at a Universal level or that one or more of the participants is not aligned with that purpose.

Whether or not there is alignment with purpose, it is always appropriate for the participants to express unconditional love and support for each other.

Let me define unconditional love and support. It means

allowing the person to be perfect just the way she is. We see beyond the way a person is outwardly expressing to her essence. We honor the essence as the true being. This is all done at the consciousness level.

Do not confuse unconditional love and support with the need to *do* anything outwardly. It doesn't mean the obligation to give money, spend time with someone, or do anything in particular, but it can result in an outward action. However, to be beneficial to all parties, that action is inspired and totally voluntary—not done out of a sense of obligation.

In summary then, the definition and re-definition of group purpose is the single most valuable activity for any group to experience. Having an inspiring group purpose and re-defining it from time to time, as may be necessary, guarantees not only success for the group, but success for the participants even beyond their experience in the group.

SURRENDER

One of the ways we complicate our lives and block mastery of the life experience is by thinking that we are the source of our power. So strong is our belief that we must continually remind ourselves that we are agents, not principals in the real game of life. It is only when we realize that the Universe works through us and provides us with Its power, that life becomes simple, easy and successful.

When we are willing to surrender to the inherent perfection of the Universe and let It flow through us, we shall achieve the very results to which we aspire.

The opportunity to live our lives is the greatest privilege we have. Following the basic laws of the Universe leads us to a life of total and complete joy in every moment. Like any privilege, to be enjoyed, it must first be cherished. Each of us has been given the keys to the kingdom. We can use them only when we remember the source of the gift.

QUIET, HARMONY AND RHYTHM

There is a basic rhythm to the Universe. We can notice it only when we are quiet enough to listen. Each of us has a rhythm that is in natural harmony with the universal rhythm. All of us together have rhythms that are in harmony with each other and with the Universe. We have to be quiet to hear and feel these rhythms. Life is so simple when we hear, feel, and follow them. There is a rhythm to our walk, to our speech, to our eating, to our playing golf, tennis and swimming. There is a rhythm to our relating to others.

The Infinite Intelligence of the Universe is behind these rhythms. As we become more and more sensitive to them, we pick up the natural guidance that is there for us, at all times.

The world of illusion, with its customary disrespect for what is natural, simple, and easy, creates so much background noise, that it impedes our ability to hear and feel these rhythms. As we become more sensitive to them, we will attract a more peaceful environment in which to live our lives.

As we practice being quiet, we hear and feel the rhythms in us and around us, and then we notice the magnificent harmony of the Universe.

UNCOVERING JOY

Any part of our lives which we perceive as less than perfect is an illusion. The infinite supply of energy from the Universe is not available to support illusions; they require our own energy to keep them alive. This is why dealing with illusions is so tiring.

Yet releasing illusions from our consciousness is only part of the solution. It is important that we replace what we have released with something that we prefer. Thus we must focus our attention on the quality of life that we desire. Quality of life is really the *feeling* that is the setting for the events and people that pass through our lives. If we are feeling wonderful, we don't really care who we are with, where we are, or what is going on. What's more, *we control how we feel all of the time*.

The only *real* feeling we ever have is joy. That is a part of our essence, the only *real* part of us. *Our function is to keep reminding ourselves of the difference between what is real in our lives and what is an illusion.* An important part of that function is rediscovering our inner joy. Most of us have buried the joy below layers and layers of illusory feelings. It is necessary to keep peeling them off until the joy is uncovered and allowed to fill our being.

There is no substitute for this procedure, no shortcuts. It is a truly personal experience for each of us. No one can do it for another person. All we can do is support a person who is doing it for himself.

The principles discussed in this book are the intellectual justification for believing that only our joy is real. Using the principles enables us to release the joy within

Of one thing we can be certain: joy will always be there, in us, and in everyone else.

The quality of our lives then depends upon:

> The degree to which we are willing to recognize that the only feeling that is real is joy.

> The degree to which we are willing to release the joy within.

> The degree to which we recognize that the only obstacle to releasing joy is the unwillingness to express love for someone or something.

A good way to practice locating the joy is to do the IDEAL DAY EXERCISE.[39] Since what we focus thought on expands, the more we look for, think about and uncover the joy within, the more real it becomes for us. There is no other way to do this. If we wish to achieve a life of joy, we have to continually practice experiencing joy. The means and the end are always identical. *You achieve joy by being joyful.*

THE THREE STEP
A NEW DANCE OF LIFE

Whenever anything occurs that creates discomfort in your body, remind yourself of the following:

Whatever you are experiencing is what you have created. However you are feeling is how you *want* to feel.

Do not judge yourself, anyone else, or the event you are experiencing. In the event you realize you are judging anyone, begin the practice of forgiveness. Daily, in the quiet of your room, bring the person you are judging into your consciousness. Feel yourself forgiving him. Also forgive yourself for judging him and for judging yourself. Continue with this practice on a daily basis until you notice that you have released all judgment. Then feel unconditional love for the person and yourself. Continue until you feel love easily, just at the mention of the person's name. Be patient. Allow as long as you need to comfortably release all judgment, and feel love. Do not make time a factor. Be gentle and kind to yourself as you do this.

Ask yourself, "How would I like to feel?" Focus on feeling as wonderful as you possibly can. Use whatever techniques you can to locate the inner joyfulness and allow it to fill your being. By practicing the IDEAL DAY EXERCISE every day, you prepare yourself for this third and vital step.

As you learn to make this three step procedure a habit, you will achieve the sense of how easy it is to have your life the way you wish it to be. You will realize that all that is left between you and a perfect life of total joyfulness, is your willingness to allow yourself to *have* it.

WE START FROM COMPLETION

We cannot enjoy our lives to the fullest unless we are experiencing the total joy that is an expression of our real selves.

In order to experience total joy, we must feel complete and live fully in the present moment. We need *do* nothing to achieve a life that works perfectly. It is a gift from the Universe. In other words, we start out being whole and complete. Everything is always provided for us. The reason we are without anything is because we believe we cannot have it at that moment, or more accurately stated, we really do not *want* it.

Remember, having, believing, and wanting are synonymous. That is the law of cause and effect. If we do not *have* anything we think we *want*, it is only because we do not *really* want it. Abundance is the natural state of affairs in the Universe. It wants to flow through our lives. When we are not enjoying total abundance in each and every aspect of our lives, it is only because we are pushing it away.

When we realize that we were given a life of perfection we can relax, allowing the inner joyfulness that is our real self to emerge and fill our beings. Every time we try to feel better by changing anything in the world around us, we deny the truth that we are already perfect.

The one thing that each of us has total control over is how we *feel* at any given moment. We can choose to feel any way we wish at any time. When we choose to feel happy, we attract only happiness into our lives.

Life is always the way we view it. It is a perceptual experience. Perceive it as perfect and it is perfect. Perceiving it as anything other than perfect is an illusion. The more we believe that the world of illusion is real, the more chaos and pain we create in our lives.

As stated many times before, do not be misled by the simplicity of it all. The Universe, in Its infinite wisdom, is an experience of simplicity at all times. It takes Infinite Intelligence to create true simplicity. Believe it! Enjoy it! And then, you do have it all!

NOTES

1. See chapter on THE UNIVERSE for definition of intuition, page 15.
2. See chapter on PURPOSE, page 25.
3. See chapter on ENERGY, page 9.
4. See chapter on HARMONY, page 83.
5. This is the definition given me by Phil Laut, author of *Money is My Friend*.
6. See chapter on DOING WHAT WE LOVE, page 35.
7. See chapter on ENERGY, page 9.
8. For details on how we can use the law of cause and effect to our benefit, see chapter on HOW TO CHANGE WHAT WE WANT, page 137.
9. See chapter on ENERGY, page 9.
10. For ways to change the signals we emit, see chapters on HOW TO CHANGE WHAT WE WANT, page 137, RELEASING PROBLEMS, page143 and UNCOVERING JOY, page 175.
11. See chapter on THE PAST AND FORGIVENESS, page 85.
12. See chapter on AWARENESS, page119.
13. See chapter on ENERGY, page 9.
14. See chapter on DOING WHAT WE LOVE, page 35.
15. See chapter on WAYS TO GENERATE MORE ABUNDANCE, page 145.
16. See chapter on ABUNDANCE, page 49.
17. See chapter on SUPPORT, page 153.
18. See chapter on ENERGY, page 9.
19. See chapter on MEDITATION, page 149.
20. See chapter on YOUR IDEAL DAY EXERCISE, page111.
21. See chapter on EMOTIONS, page 79.

22. See chapter on EMOTION, page 79.
23. See chapter on THE PAST AND FORGIVENESS, page 85.
24. See chapter on MEANS AND ENDS, page 141.
25. See chapter on PERFECTION, page 31.
26. See chapter on SUPPORT, page 153.
27. See chapter on PERFECTION, page 31.
28. See chapter on ABUNDANCE, page 49.
29. See chapter on ABUNDANCE, page 49.
30. See chapter on THERE IS NO RIGHT & WRONG, page 75.
31. See chapter on YOUR IDEAL DAY EXERCISE, page 111.
32. See chapter on DETAILS, page 69
33. See chapter on EMOTION, page 79.
34. Guidelines for the INTUITIVE DIALOGUE are set forth later in this chapter.
35. See chapter on PURPOSE, page 25.
36. See chapter on SUPPORT, page 153.
37. See chapter on THE THREE STEP—A NEW DANCE OF LIFE, page 177.
38. See chapter on YOUR IDEAL DAY EXERCISE, page 111.
39. See chapter on YOUR IDEAL DAY EXERCISE, page 111.

**FOR INFORMATION ABOUT WORKSHOPS
AND BOOKS, WRITE:**

**CELEBRATION PUBLISHING
BOX 336
PIERMONT, NEW YORK 10968**